MAKING THE CASE

Using Case Studies for Teaching and Knowledge Management in Public Administration

Andrew Graham

Queen's Policy Studies Series
School of Policy Studies, Queen's University
McGill-Queen's University Press
Montreal & Kingston • London • Ithaca

Queen's University

SCHOOL OF
Policy Studies

Publications Unit
Robert Sutherland Hall
138 Union Street
Kingston, ON, Canada
K7L 3N6
www.queensu.ca/sps/

The preferred citation for this book is:
Graham, A. 2011. *Making the Case: Using Case Studies for Teaching and Knowledge Management in Public Administration*. Montreal and Kingston: Queen's Policy Studies Series, McGill-Queen's University Press.

Library and Archives Canada Cataloguing in Publication

Graham, Andrew (Andrew Bryan)
Making the case : using case studies for teaching and knowledge management in public administration / Andrew Graham.

(Queen's policy studies series)
Includes bibliographical references.
ISBN 978-1-55339-302-3

1. Public administration—Study and teaching (Higher). 2. Knowledge management—Study and teaching (Higher). 3. Public administration—Case studies. 4. Knowledge management—Case studies. I. Queen's University (Kingston, Ont.). School of Policy Studies II. Title. III. Series: Queen's policy studies series

JF1338.A2G73 2011 351.071'1 C2010-907405-X

Contents

Preface

This short text on case studies is the product of an amazing collaboration and a few accidental opportunities along the way. Teaching at the School of Policy Studies, Queen's University, I realized the real learning benefits of the case study approach, taken, as the saying goes, in moderation. As a long-serving public executive in government I also came to realize the need to share experience in that fast-paced world to either avoid reinventing the wheel or learn from others how to make a wheel better suited to your purposes. I came to see case studies as a valuable tool in such a process. And so began the writing and collecting of case material for my own teaching use.

Then, as chance and opportunity often present themselves, along came Gabe Sakaly, CEO of the Institute of Public Administration of Canada (IPAC), a long-time colleague across governments, looking for a new editor for the IPAC Case Study Series. As I took on that role, I began to see the potential for broadening the case inventory and increasing its accessibility. Re-enter change and opportunity with a visit from the Canada School of Public Service (CSPS) to Queen's to suggest a partnership with them in their Brazil-Canada Governance Capacity Project. I took on the principal coordination role for Queen's, and the project moved ahead. I have to thank the great folks in the International Section of CSPS, most notably Ian Creery, Richard Hookham, and Adrienne Jack, for a real collaborative effort and for encouraging us into new fields of collaboration. The final entrance to this series of changes and opportunities was ENAP, the Brazilian School of Public Administration. Under the direction of Helena Carr, Paula Montinger, and Elizabete Ferrarezi, ENAP had begun the development of a case series designed for use in its extensive professional development programming. Through them I developed and taught two workshops on case studies methodology for ENAP and its partner universities.

I want to thank each of these individuals for their friendship, inspiration, and guidance.

This brings us to this book. I claim no deep expertise here. Case studies are clearly understood in different ways by different people. My hope is to bring to the Canadian scene some more structured thinking about them. As well, I want to broaden their use and see them not just as classroom tools but as an important contribution to what we call knowledge management within public sector organizations. In fact, my own view is that cases are tangible means of sharing knowledge in a very hands-on, practical way.

As I also want to avoid reinventing the wheel, I draw on the expertise of others around the world. I sincerely hope that I have both acknowledged and recognized their contributions sufficiently and fairly.

I also want to thank the relentless but inspired editing of Ellie Barton. She uncovered more than one flaw in the logic and more than one failure to reference text properly. A special thanks goes to Mark Howes and Val Jarus of the School's publications unit, who were always ready to help and expedite the process.

Part 1

Using, Writing, and Teaching Case Studies in Public Administration

CHAPTER 1

INTRODUCTION: WHY CASE STUDIES? WHY NOW?

> *Case instructors often say, "There is no right answer to a case." What is more accurate to say is that there might be many right answers.*
>
> – Robert Bruner[1]

We live in times of significant demographic and technological transition in government and the broader public sector. People are leaving. New people are arriving. The swirl of senior leaders continues unabated. In their wake, they leave memory gaps; with them they take accumulated experience. What about that experience and the wisdom it can offer others? Gone in the tail stream of business. Retired or moved on.

With all the technological advances, we are constantly moving more and more information around. Yet as decentralized databases replace hard-copy filing systems, most governments have lost a lot of institutional memory. Databases are good in themselves, faster, deeper. But where are the stories? Where is the nuance?

The richness of public organizational life does not lie in its databases. It lies in its people, their stories, how they confronted issues, either successfully or less so. So, too, for the richness of the study of public policy and management. Nothing happens in a vacuum. Government offers a context that is replete with complexity, drama, and ambiguity. Capturing that combination either for practice or for study is the advantage that case studies offer.

While much has been written about case studies as a teaching tool, this book aims to extend the range of their use to the realm of organizational learning. Similarly, while many cases exist for both academic and business use in the private sector, the use of cases in public administration has been more modest. This is not meant to detract from the existence for some time of such resources as the IPAC Case Study Series in Canada, the Electronic

Making the Case: Using Case Studies for Teaching and Knowledge Management in Public Administration, A. Graham. Montreal and Kingston: McGill-Queen's University Press, Queen's Policy Studies Series.

Hallway in the United States, and the ANZSOG Case Study Program in New Zealand and Australia. The ambition of this book is to broaden the base of use and application.

Case studies provide a rich tool for presenting problems in public administration, be they real or fictional, in such a way that the users (be they students, practitioners, or teachers) can derive significant benefit from them. Cases studies can cover the range of public policy and management issues in a unique way. Indeed, the workings of the policy process and the interplay of policy ideas, context, politics, and the constraining environment provide an ideal platform for case studies.

Overcoming the "Not Learned Here" Syndrome

What I have seen emerging over the past ten years of teaching and the years prior in public administration practice is an increasing understanding that it pays to learn from others. While every situation has unique features and challenges, the experience of one agency, department, or government can inform the decisions confronting another one. I have also observed that people learn best when they see the context of what they are reading – when they understand the interpersonal play and the underlying forces driving an organization in a certain direction. There is much to be learned from others, although we might resist this form of learning. There is a sort of "Not Learned Here" syndrome: people believe that simply looking around and sharing experiences should not inform their own decision-making because, well, it was Not Learned Here. That sort of hubris invites many public organizations to take on yet again the exercise of inventing a wheel that others have already crafted.

Cases can take the place of forms of interaction – conferences, casual discussions, and reflective retreats – that seem to be falling away owing to budget restraints and a general increase in organizational churn. Of course, case studies cannot fully replace these interactions, but they can help prevent the loss of memory and preserve the sharing of experiences. For students in a policy or management class in a school of public administration, cases provide context and nuance that, while often challenging for those who lack experience, reflect the realities of public administration more accurately than purely theoretical discourse.

Case studies as a form of assertive inquiry: Case studies encourage assertive inquiry whose aim is "to learn about the salient data and causal maps baked into another person's model, then use the insight gained to fashion a creative resolution of the conflict between that person's model and your own."

– R. Martin, *The Opposable Mind* (Boston: Harvard Business School Press), 27.

There is a crying need today for public organizations to pass on their experiences – good, bad, and otherwise – to the emerging generation of new leaders. The sharing of know-how in a less structured fashion, through what we might call relational osmosis or just being around people with more experience, is truncated by the fact that proximity is increasingly defined as a text message. And, of course, the people with considerable background and history are leaving the public service as they age and become eligible for a well-deserved retirement. Only a few are brave enough to take up a new career in teaching, as rewarding as that is. Those of us who do so soon learn, however, that the informal sharing of experience that worked well in the trenches does not translate as well to the classroom. Case studies provide a format for communicating experiences – one that combines know-how with academic theory and teaching methodology. Case studies demonstrate the applicability of public administration theory. They lead to broader application of the experience, the derivation of lessons learned, and the potential for decision-making.

Case Studies around the World

This book began its life as a guidebook developed for a workshop on the case study methodology, taught at ENAP, the National School of Public Administration of Brazil. I was invited to give this workshop through the sponsorship of the Canadian International Development Agency (CIDA) and the Canada School of Public Service. The workshop was part of a broader partnership in the exchange of emerging teaching methodologies between Canada and Brazil. The area of case studies had been identified by ENAP as one of great potential interest. After a research seminar at Queen's University in partnership with the Institute of Public Administration of Canada (IPAC), which explored potential uses of case studies, a joint effort was undertaken to build the workshop and material for it.

The workshop was a great success in that it provided a new set of materials on case studies, one focused entirely on the public sector, to a range of teachers and practitioners from ENAP and a number of its partner government schools across Brazil. What became clear through this process was a strong desire to find tools to bridge the theoretical and the practical without discounting the value of either. Further, there was a desire to start a process of documenting the public administration experience in a way that would be useful to both academics and practitioners. Undergirding this tableau was an emerging belief that the real experiences of actors within the public domain need to be better shared.

The public sector around the world is in a state of flux. Governments and their agencies are trying to find innovative methods to address problems. They are also seeking to learn from other public sector experiences, whether in developed or developing countries. There is no such thing as the best practice or the one way to do things, in such a search. The challenges of public policy and management are a Rubik's Cube, not a three-dimensional field. It is invaluable to see how others address issues that resonate within one's own range of experience.

Through work with the Commonwealth Secretariat on building case studies in innovations in public sector financial management, I learned another valuable lesson: the transfer of knowledge is a two-way street. Case studies help transcend the traditional view that developed countries have a lot to give and all the rest have a lot to receive. For example, people in the United Kingdom learned participatory budgeting – how to involve citizens in decisions about allocating scarce financial resources – from people in communities in Brazil.

Finally, case studies can provide learning and analytical challenges from different eras. It has been said that we ignore history at our peril and, in doing so, are condemned to repeat it. For that reason, a case called *Launch the Vasa*, based on an event that took place almost 400 years ago, is presented in Part Two as an example of how to bridge time. It is noteworthy that this case study was developed by the National Aeronautics and Space Agency (NASA), an organization obviously focused on the future. NASA is committed to learning, and to using a case approach, with a lively sense of style.

The Canadian Perspective: The IPAC Case Study Series

There is a long history of developing case studies in Canada. The IPAC Series, of which I am currently the editor, has been in existence for almost 40 years. It has an inventory of just over 160 cases and more than 25 simulations. These case studies are primarily used for academic teaching in schools of public administration across the country. Many of the cases, while dated, have continuing relevance to public administration. Reading them is a humbling reminder that the fundamentals of public administration have not changed, but have just been renamed or repackaged.

In response to increasing interest, the focus of the series is shifting to organizational learning – the transfer of lessons learned, good practice, and wise caution and experience from one organization or generation to another. IPAC has also realized that it has a valuable source of ideas for these through its award programs and essay contests. The value-added here is that, beyond recognition of an achievement for an organization and the consequent plaque on the wall, a case study is an actual knowledge-transfer tool that enhances the meaning of the award. It supports the sustainability of excellence.

In Canada, governments are increasingly using case studies for learning as well as for documenting the significant challenges they have faced. Both at the federal and provincial levels, projects have been launched to build case studies that address the learning objectives of those governments. This is a departure for government, one that requires considerable foresight in terms of documenting cases that reflect not just the positive but also the negative and contentious. How these projects evolve will probably be a case in itself.

The Future of Case Studies

Stories will never stop – they are the life blood of human interaction. What is happening, however, is that stories are going online into social networks and other emerging media. Case studies, too, are going online. Public sector providers of case studies, such as IPAC in Canada and the Electronic Hallway in the United States, are converting their case resources into electronic resources and increasingly making their services more of a portal than an inventory.

Social networking is just another way to share stories. Organizations are beginning to realize that with adequate safeguards, social media can be a powerful way to pass on ideas, lessons learned, and practical tips. A good example of that is the knowledge gateway of Natural Resources Canada. This is an internal social media platform for the sharing of experiences and ideas among the scientists, policy analysts, and administrative support staff of this federal government department. It has fostered new forms of collaboration and permitted the sharing of information on a fully networked basis.

Another example is the emergence of new sites to share case studies across specific fields. One such site is CaseStudiesOnline.com. Although restricted in scope to social media in the private sector, it points to the ease with which cases can be shared, searched, and integrated into other business activities.

The Search for a Template

Much is written in this book about how to write a case study. But I have often been asked, "Where is the template that I need to fill in?" Indeed, templates come in many different formats and are available online in many places. I will not suggest one single template, because the range is just too broad. There is ample information here to help writers or organizations design a template if that is something that they see as important. Many organizations do design templates so that they can present their cases studies in a common format. Templates also discipline length and force the writer to address certain issues.

The Ethics of Case Studies

Both writing and teaching cases demand an ethical approach, one that respects the privacy of those involved and ensures that the information or ideas portrayed are properly attributed. There are no set ethical standards in place for case studies. There is no enforcement of any kind, except that imposed by organizations adopting and distributing cases. A quick scan will reveal, however, that the term *case study* is used loosely. It may not be unethical, but it can be misleading for companies to claim that their products have been validated by case studies. A sentence or two about a well-executed project might make for good publicity, but does not constitute a true case study. However, in the absence of any strictures upon usage, these organizations are free to use any term they choose. *Caveat emptor.*

For the cases dealt with in this book, there are a number of ethical issues that suggest the adoption of cautionary practices in the areas of

- Research and information gathering
- Identification of actors
- Attribution and permission
- Review and validation processes – peer review equivalents

Ethical Risks in Case Studies

Those who prepare and use case studies make up a varied group. They are intersectoral (governmental, academic, commercial, voluntary, and non-profit) and interdisciplinary (sociology, psychology, economics, politics, marketing, social work, etc.). They are international and multi-problem based. Any attempt to limit the interests of practitioners or the tools they use would be a waste of time and a restraint on creativity. Many who produce cases already work within the ethical framework of their profession, such as academics. They are also constrained by governmental requirements for privacy and the protection of personal and secure information.

Therefore it is not necessary to create a new framework of ethics. What is needed is a reminder that cases do pose some special ethical challenges. Case studies do not need to pass the test of academic peer review, nor are they likely to be put to any evidentiary test in the courts. In fact, it is in the nature of case studies to be stories – to use selective information, fictional or factual, to achieve certain learning ends. One of the advantages of case studies over formal reports, studies, or evaluations is that their focus on problem solving and knowledge transfer permits considerable flexibility. Such an advantage also can create problems.

Some of the ethical risks inherent in case studies are

- Converting factual situations into fictional ones for the purposes of the case, but failing to protect the identity of the actors
- Confusing fact with fiction or implying that fiction is fact
- Misquoting people
- Falsely attributing motives, especially in factual cases
- Needlessly criticizing an actor

- Using cases to advance causes or products without disclosing funding or obligations to those causes or products
- Using cases to damage the reputations of people or organizations

Guidelines for the Ethical Use of Cases

Given the variety of sources and forms of case studies, it is impossible to be definitive in what an ethical approach would entail. However, certain general principles do apply. The following are suggested guidelines to take into account when both writing and teaching cases.

Clarity on sponsorship. If the case is written with the sponsorship of an organization or firm, both the nature of that sponsorship and the degree of content control should be declared. The degree of control or editorship should be clarified in advance of the research.

Research ethics. Those being interviewed for a case should understand the intent of the questioning. Every effort should be made to inform those interviewed of questions or lines of inquiry in advance. In some instances, informed consent should be documented.

Review or quality control. Some form of peer or editorial review that provides a quality and use check is desirable but not always practical.

Obligations to subjects. There should be fair disclosure of the subject's identity in factual cases. In fictionalized cases based on real-life situations, every effort should be made to protect the identity of subjects. Writers of case studies should respect their subjects, and avoid inflammatory characterization or speculation about motives.

Disclosure of use. All those involved in the research should be made aware of the anticipated uses of the cases (e.g., publication, posting, formal or informal, restricted or freely available).

Clarity on sources. The author should state whether the case is fictional, fictionalized, or factual.

Documentation of sources. The use of primary and secondary materials should be documented. Quotations from interview subjects should be validated, especially if there is personal attribution. Case writers should protect their notes from unintended usage.

Note

[1] R. R. Bruner, "The Role of the Student in the Case Method Classroom," http://faculty.dareden.virginia.edu/brunerb/case-student.htm.

Chapter 2

Case Studies: Definitions, Uses, Resources, and Potential

Every case is as different as the people to whom it happened.

– Barnes, Christensen, and Hansen[1]

Case studies represent a valuable resource for teaching and learning, not just for the traditional teaching environment but also for the purposes of organizational learning and knowledge transfer. While the use of case studies in public administration has been limited, it is growing; indeed, case studies are becoming increasingly relevant. For one thing, case studies are designed to bring out details from the multiple viewpoints of those involved. For both teaching and understanding complex public issues, this complexity is closer to the reality of the situation than linear or one-dimensional portrayals of policy and public service issues.

The purposes of this overview are fourfold:

1. To assess the relative state of public administration case studies
2. To propose a working definition and typology of case studies
3. To describe the various uses of case studies for public administration[2] purposes
4. To suggest topical areas for the development of new case studies

Scanning the Environment

This chapter is actually an environmental scan of sorts. It was created through the cooperation of many teachers and practitioners in Canada and around the world. It is intended to stimulate further discussion about how case studies can advance both good teaching and effective organizational learning through the experience of others. There has been increased interest in the use of case studies for various forms of learning. The reasons for this

Making the Case: Using Case Studies for Teaching and Knowledge Management in Public Administration, A. Graham. Montreal and Kingston: McGill-Queen's University Press, Queen's Policy Studies Series.

appear to be both academic and practical, as reflected by the trends that emerged from this scan:

- A strong desire to match theoretical learning with practical application[3]
- The growth in the number of public policy and administration programs in Canada
- A shifting demographic within the public sector
- A growing recognition that the challenges faced by one organization have striking parallels in others
- The increasingly global nature of knowledge sharing

These trends point to the growing relevance of case studies. The increased number of public policy and administration programs broadens the variety of teaching methodologies used, including the greater application of case studies. The approaching retirement of a generation of leaders from the public sector makes it desirable, and in some cases necessary, to find a means to transfer experience and knowledge to the next generation. Case studies provide a structure for passing on this experience. Likewise, organizations can learn from the approaches taken by others. Whether an approach fits perfectly or not, there are lessons to be learned from hits and misses on a performance target. As knowledge sharing becomes increasingly global, there is a fruitful field for exchanging experiences through case studies.

Despite the potential of case studies as a learning and knowledge-sharing tool, there has been very little systematic application of case studies within government organizations. Case studies are used sporadically, or not at all, in formal training programs offered by governments and professional institutes. Even at a time when governments are losing people with know-how, sharing and disseminating cases among practitioners is not seen as a priority. Why? I believe people lack an awareness of how to write and teach cases. What's more, there is a shortage of cases on public policy issues. A number of case studies have been published on websites, and many are listed at the end of this chapter and in the inventory at the end of this book. But most of these cases focus on management issues, issues of public engagement, and responses to emergency or crisis situations. Cases on policy and policy formulation are less prevalent. Moreover, websites are a passive modality. What is needed are methodologies for using case studies in the public sector for teaching and learning.

Working Definition of a Case Study

Before we consider ways to use case studies, a working definition is needed. Case studies can serve many purposes, but they tend to have some common elements:

- An anecdotal element
- Documentation of real or fictional issues

- Focus on a problem or challenge, either presenting a problem to resolve or documenting the subject's efforts to resolve it
- A heavy focus on context and mitigating circumstances
- The potential for the transfer of knowledge, understanding, or skills through the case to students, practitioners, or researchers

A case study is a triangulation of people, events, and circumstances. It presents a public policy or administration problem in the form of a story, combined with contextual and background information, in such a way that users can draw conclusions about public sector theory, potentially improve existing practice, consider and evaluate alternative responses to the situation, and enhance their understanding of the circumstances in which decisions were made. But a case is more. It is also a structured way in which to share experience, reveal challenges and opportunities that an organization has faced, share lessons learned and leading practices that might help other in similar situations.

The same case study can be used in many ways: teaching, learning, and identifying leading practice, and documenting lessons learned or practical tips.

To that end, many cases, especially those for teaching, are not meant to convey the complete set of facts but rather a select number of them. For the most part, they do not tell the whole story. Instead of offering a definitive version of history, case studies challenge users to add their own interpretations to an incomplete body of knowledge. Case studies present a learning scenario that mirrors real life, where decisions are made and conclusions reached based on partial information, ideological orientations, and preset assumptions about what is and is not known. Users of case studies are forced to make assumptions about the underlying thinking or background in the case, just as they do when confronted with imperfect information in real life. Users also have to deal with the ambiguities of a situation. It is often in the clarification process that the best learning takes place.

Toward a Typology for Case Studies

It is important in developing a perspective on the case study method to recognize its diversity and complexity. Case studies can range in length and complexity from a paragraph to a 100-page narrative. However, the method represents a positive opportunity to enhance understanding of theory, share and understand the experience of others in a way that such experience can be translated into a different context, and build a body of knowledge about an issue to permit further theoretical and practical analysis. The typology shown in Figure 2.1 helps us to see the range of materials and formats that cases can usefully take for practitioners, students, teachers, and researchers.

FIGURE 2.1
A Typology for Case Studies

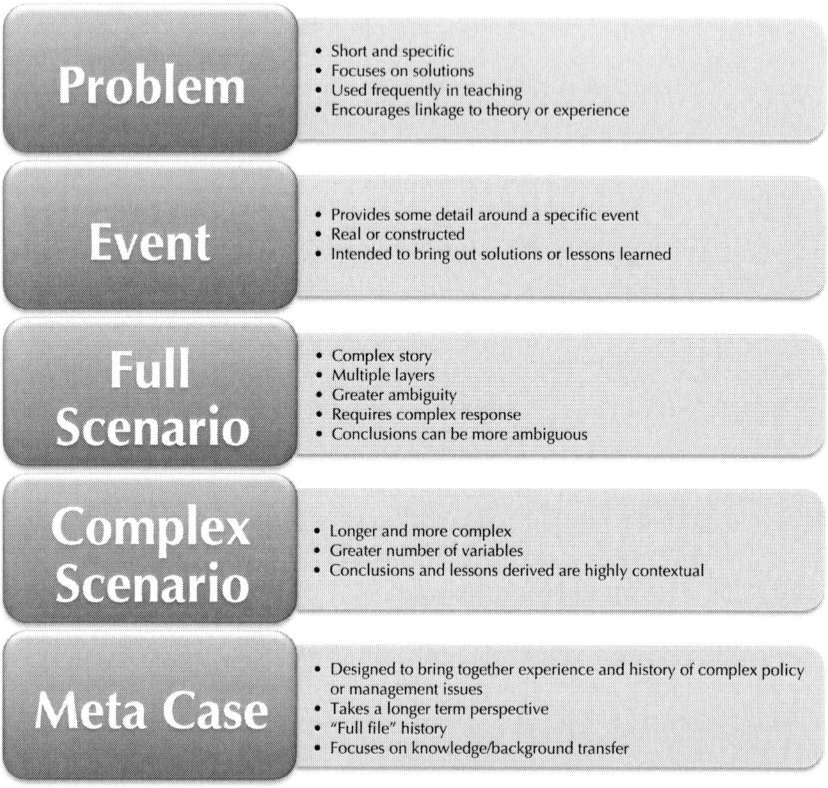

Who Makes Use of Case Studies, and Why?

For the *student* of public administration, a case study represents the opportunity to apply theory to practice, increase analytical skills, work with others, and communicate potential solutions to problems of public administration. For the *researcher*, the case study permits the investigation and assembly of information associated with a specific public administration or policy problem through a methodology that marries empirical data with the contextual factors that affect the relevance and impact of the information.

> *There has been an increase in interest in case studies for both practitioners and teachers.*

For the *practitioner*, a case study permits the transfer of organizational knowledge either within an organization or across public sector organizations (see Figure 2.2). Case studies document an organization's experience with a specific challenge in such a way that practitioners can see the facts and context associated with certain practices, and how well those practices worked.

FIGURE 2.2
Users and Uses of Case Studies

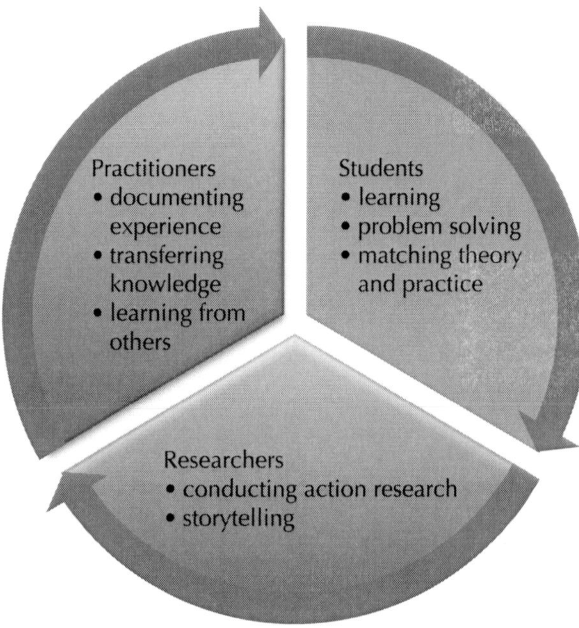

Different Uses of the Case Study Method

Table 2.1 outlines the three key functions that case studies can usefully serve. While no hard borders exist among the functions, cases can serve a variety of functions. The focus of this book is clearly on teaching and organizational learning, and much will be said about these in subsequent chapters. Some commentary of the use of case studies in research is offered in this section.

Teaching. Case studies can be used in the classroom to simulate either real or fictional events that students attempt to resolve by applying theory, analysis, and problem-solving tools – all for learning purposes. This is perhaps the most commonly thought-of use for case studies.

Organizational learning. Case studies are used by organizations to share experiences in a variety of challenges, outline leading practice, and understand vulnerabilities and errors. Case studies are a dynamic means of evaluating existing practice; this use is less formal than program evaluation and closer to practice-sharing.

Research. For research purposes, case studies are used to document an event, a series of events, or a policy issue. Both the facts and context in which the problem has evolved are documented; the purpose is to develop, through a case approach, the background and reasons for developments as they occurred.

TABLE 2.1
Characteristics of the Case Study Method

	Teaching	Organizational Learning	Research
Source of Information	Fact or fiction	Factual with an emphasis on context	Multiple sources of information based on empirical inquiry
Learning Objectives	Specific learning objectives – often linked to theory	Transfer of knowledge, know-how, practice, and experience	Provide research results
Formats	Wide range of formats to suit teaching situation	Documents practices and lessons learned	Lengthier with more detail to substantiate findings
General Approach	Draws out lessons relevant to teaching objectives	Focus on lessons learned and understanding both facts and context	Designed to substantiate or disprove opening assumptions
Individual Benefits	Develops skills, e.g., analysis, group work, communication, problem solving	Sharing of practice, documentation of results, avoiding further error	Give substance to research objectives in narrative form
Distinguishing Characteristics	Theory and practice combined	Strong on craft and transfer of how-to and what not to do	Triangulation of theory, subject, and context

Case Studies for Research

The remaining chapters focus on the uses of case studies for teaching and organizational learning. Using case studies in research is a specialized topic with its own set of issues. Case study research is not dealt with extensively in this book, but merits a brief discussion here.

Case study research excels at bringing the reader to an understanding of a complex issue. It can extend experience or add strength to what is already known through previous research. Case studies emphasize detailed contextual analysis of a limited number of events or conditions and their relationships. Researchers have used the case study research method for many years across a variety of disciplines. Social scientists, in particular, have made wide use of this qualitative research method to examine contemporary real-life situations and provide the basis for the application of ideas and extension of methods. Researcher Robert K. Yin defines the case study research method as an empirical inquiry that uses multiple sources of evidence to investigate a contemporary phenomenon within its real-life context, when the boundaries between phenomenon and context are not clearly evident.[4]

Critics of the case study method believe that the study of a small number of cases can offer no grounds for establishing reliability or generality of findings; they can be readily dismissed as merely anecdotal. Others feel that the intense exposure to study of the case biases the findings in that the case approach will seek to document contextual matters as well as structured data. Some dismiss case study research as useful only as an exploratory tool from which firm conclusions cannot be reached.

Case studies are in fact less rigorous than surveys or other research methods. They are driven often by narrative lines or qualitative over quantitative research. In conducting and writing case studies, researchers should use care in being systematic in their data collection and take steps to ensure validity and reliability in the study. Researchers continue to use the case study research method with success in carefully planned and crafted studies of real-life situations, issues, and problems. Reports on case studies from many disciplines are widely available in the literature.

Public Administration Case Study Resources

The range of case study resources principally falls within the following categories:

1. Case study texts
2. Portal-type websites
3. Specialized websites, often operated by specialist organizations within the public sector

Websites that focus entirely on public administration case studies are few indeed. But they do exist, and delving into their inventories will reveal very useful and applicable case studies. A global scan revealed some of the most important sites. Selected sites are listed here; for a more comprehensive list, see the Inventory of Public Administration Case Study Sites at the end of the book.

International

Australia and New Zealand School of Government (ANZSOG): http://www.casestudies.anzsog.edu.au/. This is a joint effort of the governments of Australia and New Zealand. Its primary aim is to foster the creation and use of public sector case studies. Access is controlled.

European Case Clearing House: http://www.ecchatbabson.org/. This may well be the largest depository of case studies in the world. However, the focus is on business cases rather than the public sector, although there are many very good cases for use in government or about government. This is a commercial site, and cases must be purchased.

United Nations Public Administration Network (UNPAN): http://www.unpan.org. Case studies abound within the various sector reports. This is a complex site with no one source of case study material but well worth the search for specific public sector applications on cases.

United States

The Electronic Hallway: http://hallway.evans.washington.edu/. This is a partnership consortium of university partners across the United States, with some international partners and foundation support. It contains an array of pubic sector cases of exceptional quality and depth. Teaching notes are robust and useful. It is of use to teachers but also to organizations wanting to learn from the experience of others as some cases are focused on real life situations and often quite topical. Membership is required and fees were recently introduced.

Kennedy School Case Study Program, Harvard University: http://www.ksgcase.harvard.edu/. This is a well-known and high-profile source for case material. It is operated on a commercial basis. Teaching notes are of high quality.

Maxwell School of Syracuse University Collaborative Governance Initiative (CGI): www.maxwell.syr.edu/parc/eparc. This site supports the Maxwell School's work on conflict and collaboration. It is a very good example of a small number of well-chosen cases focused on conflict resolution. Cases presented were winners of an annual case contest sponsored by e-parc. This example is but one of many available in specialized institutions around the world.

Pew Case Study Program at the Georgetown School of Foreign Service: http://www12.georgetown.edu/sfs/ecase/. Once again, here is a specialized area of intellectual interest that offers case material to support its work.

United States Government Accountability Office: http://www.gao.gov/bestpractices/. The GAO produces many reports on government performance and accountability issues. Its best practices reports are an attempt to distribute information on organizational practice that could be applied outside the originating organization. These are small cases and best set in the context of knowledge sharing rather than teaching.

In addition, a number of case databases are available in specialized subject areas. An example of this is the Trade and Environment Database (TED). This database is described on the home page as "a collection of categorical case studies that began with a focus on solely environmental issues, but did not include the economic consequences of other social policy choices, such as culture, rights, or other issues." Some 700 TED cases studies are available at http://www1.american.edu/TED/ted.htm.

Canada

Institute of Public Administration of Canada Case Study Program: http://www.ipac.ca/Case_StudiesProgram. This is the premier site for Canadian teaching cases. The inventory has over 200 cases, some with teaching notes. IPAC is also developing a series of cases on international development, available at http://www.democraticdevelopment.ca/, as well as organizational learning case studies.

Ivey School of Business Case Program University of Western Ontario: www.iveycases.com. The Ivey case program has to be recognized as the most organized and influential Canadian case study undertaking. Its focus is clearly on business cases. However, it also offers training in writing and teaching cases that is of high quality.

Some Canadian Federal Government Case Sources of Interest

The Canadian federal government has no collective source of case studies for the sharing of knowledge, experience, and learning opportunities. However, a small number of case study sites are available. These tend to have certain common characteristics:

- Each site is highly specialized.
- Each site has only a small number of cases.
- Many of the cases are quite short, with little documentation and not enough to provide either for critical analysis or the transfer of lessons learned.
- The cases stand alone, usually the initiative of one agency or program, but not linked or accessible through a common portal.
- They represent the genuine efforts of the particular agency to tell their story or offer representative case information; this should be lauded.

In general, the federal government does not offer a systematic approach to case studies as a means of transferring knowledge and experience. Some exceptions are listed below. While a search for case studies will yield many hits, the substantive reality is that these lead to the same few departments and, in many cases, the so-called case studies are short, highly descriptive, and do not contain further resources. In other words, as with many firms in the private sector, the use of the term *case study* borders on publicity in place of actual substance.

Canada School of Public Service (CSPS): A search for case studies on the CSPS website reveals no one location or source for case study material. A number of cases are listed, but access is controlled. It should be noted that CSPS owns the extensive inventory of cases created in the 1980s and 1990s for teaching at its predecessor, the Canadian Centre for Management Development. This inventory, while dated, is a rich source of classroom teaching material, usually involving fictional situations relevant to management in the federal government. The inventory is still available through IPAC, which has an agreement with the federal government for the sale of these cases.

Canadian International Development Agency, case studies on the environment: http://www.acdi-cida.gc.ca/acdi-cida/acdi-cida.nsf/eng/STE-320155245-SKC.

Export Development Canada, Student Program in International Business Case Studies: http://www.edc.ca/english/student_casestudies.htm.

Natural Resources Canada, Buildings and Community Case Studies: http://canmetenergy-canmetenergie.nrcan-rncan.gc.ca/eng/buildings_communities/communities/publications.html. This site has comprehensive data on the energy inputs and outputs of most Canadian municipalities.

Public Health Agency of Canada (PHAC), Business Workplace Health Case Studies: http://www.phac-aspc.gc.ca/alw-vat/studies-etudes/canadian-eng.php. PHAC offers many different types of cases studies.

The Innovation Journal: http://www.innovation.cc/case-studies.htm. Although not a government department, this journal has a number of cases of federal government innovation.

Transport Canada, the Urban Program's Case Library: http://www.tc.gc.ca/programs/environment/utsp/casestudylibrary.htm. Transport Canada offers profiles of how Canadian communities are implementing sustainable urban transportation initiatives. The site links to over 60 case studies that feature project results, costs, policy contexts, and more. Transport Canada is a leading federal government provider of cases.

There would be merit in systematically gathering all current federal case study resources. These could then be readily linked to the IPAC Case Study Portal and the Public Policy Portal.

Specialized Public Sector Sites

A wide variety of specialist sites are available. Over 75 sites are listed in the IPAC inventory alone. It should be noted that there are only a small number of specialized Canadian sites. An important emerging source, linked to the new IPAC Case Portal, will be the Public Policy Portal, accessible at www.ppgportal.ca. However, this facility does not currently have unique case resources, and the overall intent is to build a partnership with IPAC in the case area.

What Resources Need to Be Developed?

A review of current inventories within some of the broadly based case websites indicates that many topics have been covered. Cases range from complex policy challenges to managerial issues of a very specific nature. Once the learning objectives are understood, generally a case can be found to be of use in the circumstances. However, some challenges persist with what is now available:

The challenge of applicability. While cases document real or fictional situations, it is sometimes difficult for users to apply them in their own circumstances, especially where the legal and cultural framework are vastly different. For example, many cases from the United States involve federal, state, or city environments totally different from countries in the Westminster system.

The challenge of timeliness. Cases age and circumstances change. While the essence of the case may be sound, there is tremendous distraction in arcane language, insensitivity to gender role changes and, in particular, changes in technology. For example, cases involving the exchange of information in the pre-BlackBerry age have an arcane, near bucolic view of the speed of information flow.

The challenge of adaptability. Cases that claim to present best practice fail to recognize that a really successful practice in one instance can be a recipe for disaster in another. Perhaps the best examples of this are efforts to use private sector cases in public sector situations.

The challenge of not invented here. In terms of organizational learning and knowledge transfer, this is perhaps the greatest challenge. Cases must have the capacity to be relevant in a variety of situations, or otherwise need to be adaptable to those circumstances. For example, a case that elicits a comment like "that would never happen here" fails the relevance test.

Therefore, some of the characteristics of good cases for organizational learning are

- Relevance to the overall public administration environment
- Transferability of experience
- Balanced in terms of both the positive and negative features of the case
- Focused on lessons learned and their applicability
- Focused on solving present problems in the real environment

Some of the topics that have been identified in informal consultations that would lend themselves to the development of cases are as follows:

- Complex policy cases involving multiple stakeholders and many government agencies
- Horizontal management in general
- Procurement with following subsets: planning, safeguard and conflicts, IT procurement, procurement modernization
- Policy processing and public engagement
- Performance measurement
- Crisis and emergency management
- Emergency planning
- Risk management
- Human resource management
- Implementation
- Financial management
- Major project management
- Resource reallocation
- Major policy initiatives – telling the story

This list is hardly exhaustive. Nor was its assembly necessarily either orderly or scientific. Rather, it was based on a survey of current federal government issues, major topics at hand, and consultations with practicing public servants.

Notes

[1] L. B. Barnes, C. R. Christensen, and A. J. Hansen, *Teaching and the Case Method: Text, Cases, and Readings*, 3rd ed. (Boston: Harvard Business School Press, 1994), 142.

[2] The term *public administration* is a broad one, encompassing public sector policy and management as well as some activities in the not-for-profit sector, especially those activities that affect the public sector.

[3] See L. Caceres and S. Schwartz, *The Labour Market Experience of Recent Graduates from Masters Programs in Public Administration* (School of Public Policy and Administration, Carleton University, July 2008), accessed at www.cappa.ca.

[4] R. K. Yin, *Case Study Research: Design and Methods* (Newbury Park, CA: Sage, 1984).

CHAPTER 3

TEACHING CASES

A good case study is the vehicle by which a chunk of reality is brought into the classroom.

– Paul. R. Lawrence

The case study method is an excellent way to bring a holistic and interactive approach to teaching and learning.[1] Its main advantage is that it takes a question-oriented as opposed to a solution-based approach. A case presents the question in a specific context, often one that involves conflict or the need to reconcile or balance many variables. This complexity can increase the demands placed upon students. They have to identify the major challenge as well as the issues of theory in the case before they can formulate appropriate solutions or approaches. In other words, case studies allow students to participate in the real-life decision-making processes of public administration and policy.

Case studies are an established method of teaching in some disciplines, particularly in law, medicine, and business. But in public policy and administration, case teaching is not as widespread as its effectiveness would suggest. This is so for two reasons. First, most of those who teach or train others have learned by traditional methods – lectures, seminars, problem sets, and examinations. This is changing as more teachers develop experience in the use of cases. Second, because it is unfamiliar, the case method requires teachers and trainers to acquire new

Why cases are increasingly important in teaching public administration:
"There is a need, in this rapidly-paced technological world, for educators to continue to slow down the process and examine human, social, ethical, and political factors in designing and implementing [complex] systems."

– DeMichiell, Manning, and Reaves, "Teaching Ethics: A Case Study Approach," 9.

Making the Case: Using Case Studies for Teaching and Knowledge Management in Public Administration, A. Graham. Montreal and Kingston: McGill-Queen's University Press, Queen's Policy Studies Series.

skills and attitudes toward teaching, a process that takes the kind of time and opportunity that many do not have because of their demanding schedules.

Nonetheless, the applicability of case teaching in public administration is now being realized. There are several reasons for that:

1. The supply of cases in public administration is growing, albeit more slowly than in other academic fields of study.
2. The case method is seen as a useful addition to the spectrum of teaching methodologies.
3. The case method inherently engages the student as an active participant in the learning process.
4. For those already in public administration, using cases draws upon their experience to embellish and enrich the case.
5. The case method is a useful way to convey knowledge from one organization to another and from one generation to another.

This text takes the approach that the case method in academic and professional learning is a useful and powerful tool. It is not, however, the only tool. It is not a panacea. As Ray Heitzman observes, "This teaching approach, while carrying the potential to serve as a panacea, is not magical in the classroom unless utilized with careful planning and execution."[2] A few academic institutions have adopted the case method as the primary means of teaching. This can be restrictive, even if cases are as useful as we contend here. Learning takes place on many planes and in many ways. Successful results are more likely to be achieved if there are a variety of methodologies in play, thereby ensuring that all students find the best way for them to learn. Similarly, some subject matter is more readily conveyed through traditional means.

What the case does is bring theory to life – and life to theory. Traditional teaching is based on the lecture. Knowledge is assumed to be the sole possession of the teacher, and, via the lecture, it flows one way: from teacher to student. The case study approach assumes that both teachers and students contribute to the learning process. Although the teacher is more familiar with the material than the students, this knowledge is not regarded as definitive. Students also bring insights and understanding to the questions at hand.

Preparing Students to Use Cases

Case studies demand that students learn in ways that may not be familiar to them. Instead of passively receiving information, students become active participants in the learning process. At times they will probably have to work with others, which can be a challenge for students who prefer independent study (case studies also involve individual assignments). What's more, there is no one right answer in most cases, something that some students will find uncomfortable. Because of the ambiguity inherent in cases, students will be called upon to made decisions based on incomplete information. For all of these reasons, the first task for the teacher is to explain what cases are and how learning takes place.

As Figure 3.1 illustrates, the case study method involves a changed relationship between the teacher and the student. The student is challenged to take the analytical and decision lead. Theory and theoretical understanding come from solving a problem or analyzing various options for action; theory is not learned first and imposed on a problem. Both teacher and students assume responsibility for student learning. Knowledge and ideas flow from teacher to student, from student to teacher, and from student to student. The teacher becomes a guide in the process and not the source of the solution. For some, this is a challenge. For everyone, it involves a change in approach.

In the case study method, attention is no longer centred on the teacher at the front of the room. The student is the centre of attention; the teacher is facilitator, sharing control with class participants without giving it up. The teacher's duty is to awaken student interest, to stimulate active engagement among students, and to encourage student contributions of ideas, analyses, and conclusions. The students' duty is to accept responsibility for their own learning, to prepare and contribute, to take the chance and express their own ideas. In other words, the students' presence in the classroom makes a difference to what is learned.

FIGURE 3.1
Teacher/Student Relationship Using Cases: From Passive to Active

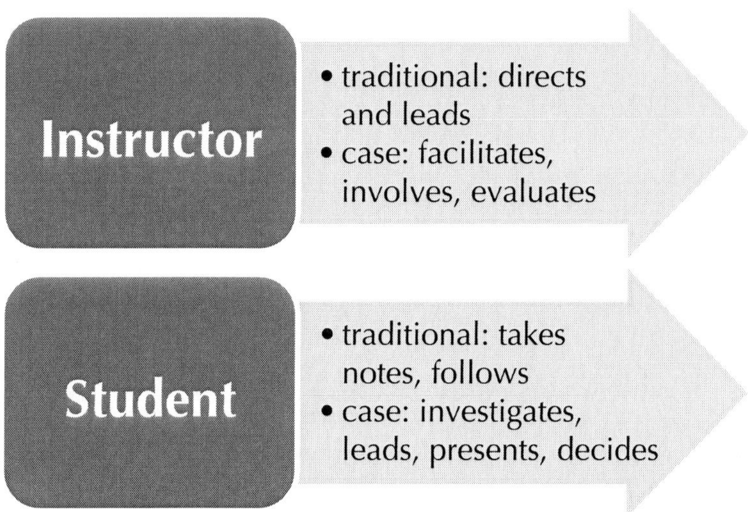

For both teachers and students, the case method is "more work but more fun." There is a premium on skill in discussion, in dealing with unexpected statements or questions, in thinking under pressure, in experimenting with ideas and solutions. Preparing for a case discussion means mental preparation and the willingness to listen to, respect, and learn from others' views. The classroom experience is not cut and dried but fluid and surprising. No two case discussions are alike, because the participants are not the same. This may be disconcerting at first to both teachers and students, because it may seem as if the discussion is out of control. Once expectations are adjusted to the assumptions underlying case teaching, however, case discussions become stimulating and rewarding.

Introducing Students to Case-Based Learning

At Harvard Medical School, incoming classes of medical students are introduced to case-based learning in three ways. First, in orientation, they do a case about plumbing (which few know about and it isn't medical, so the pressure is off). Second, also during orientation, they sit as a group of 160 in a lecture hall and watch a small group tutorial take place live in front of them (run by second year students). Third, in their first real course, time is allotted for discussing group dynamics and case processes.

You will likely want to make a low-pressure situation for your students the first time they do a case. Make it small, fun and easy, so they can learn how to brainstorm the issues and questions of the case. Don't be afraid to give explicit directions, such as:

"We begin by having one person read the case out loud. Who would like to do this?"

"Are there any words you don't know?" Or "what do you think this case is about?"

"It will help you later if one of you acts as scribe and writes down the ideas (on the chalkboard). You might want to keep track of facts, questions, issues, and proposed answers to the problem."

"We have 10 minutes left and you need to plan for next meeting. What do you see as key issues you'd like to work on?"

Students also need guidelines for how to act during discussions. Having printed guidelines can help, such as "Don't interrupt one another" ... "Don't attack people personally, focus on ideas"... "Each person must contribute to the group. There are many ways to do this."

Lifelines OnLine, "Planning for Case-Based Learning," http://bioquest.org/lifelines/PlanningStages.html. The material is excerpted from Margaret A. Waterman and Ethel D. Stanley, "Investigative Case Based Learning," a text module in the BioQUEST Library V, ed. John Jungck and Virginia Vaughan (Academic Press, 1998). Reprinted with permission.

A case discussion, then, is a learning situation. In the words of one experienced case teacher, it is "a creative preoccupation of creative minds." The goal is student competence and confidence in critical, analytical thinking and in the skills of argument and persuasion. The leader shows the path and motivates students to move along it, often from specific facts and details to general insights and conclusions. Planning and organizing the discussion are essential to the effectiveness of case teaching.

Preparing to Teach a Case

For the teacher, preparing for a case discussion means mastering the facts, issues, calculations, and other material in the case. It means trying to anticipate the questions that might arise and the arguments that might take place. (Anticipating becomes much easier with experience.) It is important to have a set of leading questions to ask should there be some hesitation at the outset or a lag in the conversation.

If the case discussion replaces the lecture as a vehicle for learning, the teacher can use a series of questions to guide students toward an understanding of the theoretical underpinnings. Alternatively, one often sees a case associated with a lecture or a set of readings. The challenge to the teacher is to ensure that they are clearly linked in the case discussion.

Instructors can write their own cases or use existing cases. The following are some things to keep in mind when creating or choosing a case:

- What do you want students to learn from the discussion of the case?
- What do they already know that applies to the case?
- What issues might be raised in discussion?
- How will you introduce the case and start the discussion?
- What preparation is expected of students? (Do they need to read the case ahead of time? Do research? Write anything?)
- What directions do you need to provide to students regarding what they are supposed to do and accomplish?
- Do you plan to divide students into groups, or will they discuss as the whole class?
- Are you going to use role-playing or facilitators or record keepers? If so, how?
- What are the opening questions?
- How much time is needed for students to discuss the case?
- What concepts are to be applied during the discussion?
- How will you evaluate students?

Cases are often accompanied by a teaching note, a plan for using the case. If there is no teaching note, teachers should prepare one. As described in *Writing Case Studies: A Manual*, a teaching note should contain a summary of the case, the learning objectives, a set of questions and an outline of how the discussion might go, tips to help students arrive at a solution, and resources such as a glossary or bibliography.[3] Writing or studying a teaching note helps teachers to visualize how they want the discussion to progress and where they want it to end up. A teaching note should be seen as an evolving tool; revising it based on the teaching experience is particularly useful.

Characteristics That Advance the Teachable Quality of a Case

A good teaching case has to present a challenging problem – a problem that is complex enough to create choices and to enable a number of possible scenarios to unfold. According to Barbara Duch of the Center for Teaching Effectiveness at the University of Delaware,

> An effective problem must first engage students' interest, and motivate them to probe for deeper understanding of the concepts being introduced. It should relate the subject to the real world, so that students have a stake in solving the problem.
>
> Good problems require students to make decisions or judgments based on facts, information, logic and/or rationalization. Students should be required to justify all decisions and reasoning based on the principles being learned. Problems should require students to define what assumptions are needed (and why), what information is relevant, and/or what steps or procedures are required in order to solve them.[4]

Purely descriptive cases provide a snapshot of an interesting or important issue, but they usually are of limited learning value. Description is only the first stage in the learning process. A bona fide teaching case should be, at a minimum, decisional and analytical. It should challenge users to move to higher orders of learning by prompting them to ask how the issues are related to one another and why things happen the way they do. Cases that document actual events may have a strong emphasis on description, but their value lies in the richness of the description and contextual information that permits the student or interested reader to understand how the case produced the results it did and to determine whether the experience would be relevant and useful in another context. In short, can we learn from this?

Cases used for teaching in public administration should encapsulate a real problem. In asking students "What are you going to do about it?" an important task for them is to define the "it." A case should draw out of students their understanding of the institutional and policy factors germane to the specific issue. For instance, an understanding of the relevant legislative process might be needed. A good case should also provide enough contextual information for students to take these factors into account in a substantive way. For example, how a similar policy issue was addressed in other countries would be relevant information. Another contextual factor might be recent shifts in principal actors in the case and the possible effects of those changes.

Case studies vary in length and in the ways information is presented, but good teaching cases will foster group activity and discussion. A good teaching case will be

- *Open-ended* – not limited to one correct answer[5]
- *Connected* to previously learned knowledge[6] that is central to the teaching objectives
- *Evocative* – elicit diverse options, perspectives, and debates
- *Relevant* to the culture, contemporary circumstances, and learning objectives at hand
- *Sustainable* – provide sufficient information, complexity, and challenge to be useful over the term of the exercise, no matter how long or short

Although cases must be sufficiently robust to forestall excessive guesswork on the part of students, good cases convey the ambiguity present in real-life public policy and administration situations. The objective is to approximate in a case the realism and tensions that face decision-makers. As one author of case studies, Paul R. Lawrence, observes,

> A good case is the vehicle by which a chunk of reality is brought into the classroom to be worked over by the class and the instructor. A good case keeps the class discussion grounded upon some of the stubborn facts that must be faced in real-life situations. It is the anchor on academic flights of speculation. It is the record of complex situations that must be literally pulled apart and put together again before the situations can be understood. It is the target for the expression of attitudes or ways of thinking brought into the classroom.[7]

Good cases, while complete for the purposes of learning, do not strive to provide all the information needed to achieve final and complete resolution of the challenges. One of the teaching challenges is to help students determine what is a sufficient response in the face of both ambiguity and incomplete information.

Teaching Cases in the Academic Setting

Case studies tend to fall into common formats, and how a case is taught will depend in part on the format. In the previous chapter, I introduced a typology for case studies that outlined five formats: problem, event, full scenario, complex scenario, and meta-case (see Figure 2.1). In this section, I expand on this basic typology, and suggest some appropriate teaching methods for each format. I have, with permission, adapted material originally prepared by BioQuest, a community of scientists and teachers interested in biology. More can be found at http://bioquest.org.

1. The Meta-Case – extensive, detailed case study

Meta-cases are frequently used in business and law courses. Meta-cases can take the form of "serial cases" in which the information unfolds over several class sessions, or they can be the central learning and analytical tool in a course. Meta-cases typically present a complex problem from a longitudinal perspective, exploring how the problem has evolved over time. These cases often centre on a detailed appreciation of the situation, the identification of interests, power relationships and underlying causes, decisions that were made, the people who made them, and the people affected by them. The cases may run from 3 to 100 pages or more.

Teaching methods. The student reads the entire case, usually individually, in advance and prepares an analysis of the decisions with recommendations for change. Longer cases benefit from group discussion, either in small groups or with the class as a whole. The challenge for the teacher is to direct the work of analysis, often by posing basic procedural questions. Given the complexity of some of these cases, and depending on how the case is to be used, the teacher may want to have a series of staged discussions to build toward a conclusion.

If the case is to be used for a written assignment, a similar process of discussion can be followed. Alternatively, class discussion can be structured with the understanding that students, or assigned groups of students, will then submit their analyses and recommendations. Regardless of the approach, the outcome will be a major review and intense group work.

2. Complex Scenario – descriptive, narrative cases that may be given successively

This style of case originated in medical school settings and is frequently used in problem-based learning. Often these cases are multidisciplinary, with no clear-cut right or wrong answer.

Teaching methods. These cases are designed to be used over the course of two or more class meetings. Often, students see the case for the first time during class. The case is disclosed to the students in stages, in tandem with the learning objectives of the session. The teacher acts as a guide, asking students to explain their thinking or to provide evidence for their ideas.

Students work collaboratively in small groups to analyze the case. As they do so, they consider what they already know and what they need to know. They generate hypotheses and develop a set of learning goals for each part of the case. Between class meetings, students look up information as they work to understand the case. The instructor's learning objectives are revealed to the student toward the end of the case. These kinds of cases are highly student directed, so they are not usually accompanied by a set of questions to be answered.

3. Problem Cases – short and specific

These are short cases, often only a paragraph or two long, describing a situation or dilemma. They do not provide much context or data, often forcing students to substitute their own interpretations of events.

Teaching methods. Designed to be used in a single class meeting, a problem case usually has tightly focused content. These cases are useful for introducing and grounding a new topic in the lecture, for pre-assessing student knowledge, for helping students apply concepts, and for introducing practical applications in lab settings. Problem cases can also be used as a pre-activity exercise designed to make the work more meaningful. These cases adapt well to distance learning when coupled with electronic discussions.

4. Problems – Bullet Cases

Two or three sentences with a single teaching point can be a case. Bullet cases are similar to problems commonly used on exams. These cases are most useful for applying concepts previously learned or for starting a new topic.

Teaching methods. Students discuss these cases briefly in small groups at the time they are introduced in class (or made available for online discussion). An example of one such problem case is "The Minister Announces." It introduces the problem of how to implement a rather sudden public policy announcement. Bullet cases are often a good way to start a discussion of a complex issue and to quickly engage students in problem-solving – one of the benefits of the case approach.

Sample Bullet Case: The Minister Announces...

Under pressure in the legislature for delays in getting disability payments to senior citizens, the Minister announced that she would reduce the process time from application to the receipt of the cheque by 50 percent in three months. She made this promise without advice from her senior administrators. You work in the Ministry that has to do this. What steps are needed to implement this?

5. Fixed-Choice Cases

These can be a variation on bullet cases above, or a mini-case with a number of plausible solutions. Multiple-choice questions can be converted easily to these if the choices are believable. The intent is to get students to consider alternative, viable solutions to a problem. Fixed-choice cases are useful for policy, ethics, and design decisions.

Teaching methods. Give the same problem and set of solutions to small groups. Each group must reach consensus on and defend one solution.

These cases make for lively in-class discussions. The example "Park That" shows how a small situation can represent a number of important dynamics such as ethics, fairness, organizational responsibility, and the fateful "telling truth to power" dilemma that can occur in any organization, but especially in the public sector.

Sample Fixed-Choice Case: Park That

The regional office for the Ministry of Social Services does not have enough parking. Buying a permit just gives staff members the right to park on a first come basis. No reservations are allowed. Recently, a sign went up reserving a space for the Regional Director. As a member of the Parking Committee (also known as the committee from hell) working in the Ministry, you must help respond to complaints that started almost immediately. Here are the proposed solutions:

1. Remove the sign and make the RD find a space like everyone else.
2. Determine why the RD needs a designated space close to the main doors. If there is a legitimate reason, let it be known. If not, remove the sign.
3. Make a two-tiered system available to all. Those who want reserved parking can pay extra for it. Others can pay less and take their chances.
4. Ignore the complaints. Everyone complains, and this is the boss after all.

What choice do you think is the best and why? How would you implement it?

An interesting teaching opportunity can arise from fixed-choice cases if students reject all the options and propose an entirely different solution. This is to be encouraged as long as the alternative view is realistic and does not create more problems than it solves.

Pedagogical Approaches

Teaching is both idiosyncratic and highly creative. No one right way exists. No single typology or description of methodologies can capture all the possibilities, and so Table 3.1 offers another way of looking at case formats and teaching methodologies. The table links the type of case with teaching objectives and learning outcomes.

TABLE 3.1
Case Categories and Approaches

Case Category	Purpose	Outcome	Integrative
Tools Cases: focusing on specific skills, issues, or questions.	Very structured and focused on applying specific skills or theories.	Solution to problem or key lessons to be derived.	Links single event or problem to skill or theory.
Decision or Prospective Cases: focusing on resolving a real or fictional challenge, often with teamwork.	Moderately structured with several pertinent factors that interconnect.	Reach a decision balancing factors applying variable analysis.	Balancing a number of variables with eye to costs and benefits of each potential course of action. The end result is unknown.
Open-Ended Cases: multiple use, often describing complex, real-life situations, sometimes as simulations.	Unstructured in the sense that many variables are at play including context, culture, and social elements.	Variables in that the first outcome is an appreciation of the situation wherein the variables are weighed, discounted, or applied. Solutions may be complex, often involving a longer-term orientation.	Significant degree of integration of non-related variables.
Meta Cases: very long, historical, and analytical.	Often complex and taking historical or longitudinal focus on specific problems in public administration, one policy area, or public management problem.	Both in teaching and organizational learning, the outcome is an understanding of the problem or issue from a historical and contextual perspective.	Tool in knowledge transfer and also in providing an up-to-date state of play in complex public policy or administration area.

Practical Steps in Building Cases into Teaching Plans

The adoption of a case methodology in teaching can be complete or episodic. An entire course or topic can be taught using only the case approach; this resembles many business schools' approach. Or, individual cases can be interspersed with other teaching tools. Either approach will work, but some basic steps have to be undertaken to ensure success. While this chapter emphasizes pedagogical approaches, it must also be remembered that students have to be equipped to successfully use case studies. More will be said about that in the next chapter.

The Interrupted Case Method

by Clyde Freeman Herreid

Far and away the most popular tactic for many faculty when teaching a case is the method of *progressive disclosure*, where the story is provided piecemeal to students, who must act as detectives to solve the mystery. This is the approach used in Problem-Based Learning (PBL) pioneered by the medical school at McMaster University. Students are given a "patient problem" and over several days are required to diagnose it as they seek information outside of class.

Here, I wish to describe a method related to PBL that I have been using for many years in classrooms and faculty development workshops. I call it the *Interrupted Case Method*. . . . Information is fed piecemeal to students working in small groups, and the Interrupted Method shares with PBL the great virtue of engaging all students in problem solving. But unlike PBL, in the Interrupted Method the case is presented in one class period rather than over several days. . . . This method of case analysis, where a problem-poser's remarks alternate with a problem-solver's remarks, can be used in the classroom in several effective ways. The most obvious but least inspired method is to use the lecture method. The teacher must develop a problem and then write the appropriate script – a dialogue between the problem-poser and the problem-solver (expert or novice). In the classroom, the instructor might present the case using the "two hat" technique – first acting as the problem-poser, and then switching hats and acting as the problem-solver. Alternatively, students could take turns reading the parts in the dialogue. This method of case presentation is largely passive, yet it does illustrate how an expert reasons his or her way through a problem. . . .

A more exciting way to use the idea is to actively involve all of the students in a problem-solving exercise using the Interrupted Case Method. Perhaps the easiest way to use the method is to select an article or case. The instructor chooses a question drawn from the introduction section of the paper. Small groups of students are asked to design an experiment to solve the problem that the article raises. After a suitable time for discussion, groups are called upon to present their experimental design and explain the reasons for their approach. Commentary is then solicited from other class members on the appropriateness of the approach.

In the next stage the instructor briefly describes how the authors of the paper decided to attack the problem. Their actual methods are described. Then the groups are asked to predict what the results might look like. Once again, groups are asked to report their solutions to the entire class with their reasoning made clear to all. Commentary from students and teacher follows.

At this point the instructor reveals the actual data published in the article. The groups are asked to interpret the results and draw conclusions in light of the original hypothesis. After a suitable discussion, the instructor reveals the author's actual interpretation of the results and their conclusions. Closure follows.

. . . [An advantage of the interrupted approach is that] it mimics how we all have to make decisions based upon incomplete data and must constantly revise our conclusions as more information becomes available.

Clyde Freeman Herreid, "The Interrupted Case Method," *Journal of College Science Teaching* 35, no. 2 (2005): 4-5, http://www3.nsta.org/main/news/stories/college_science.php?news_story_ID=51003.

The following are a number of recommended steps to build capacity to use cases in teaching:

1. Start with a simple case first. Some experts recommend using multiple cases throughout a course, so that students become more comfortable with case assignments over time. However, if only one case is possible, it is best that it not be too complex, especially in lower-level courses.
2. Take sufficient time to introduce the narrative and to establish the case facts, noting that this is only the first phase.
3. Discuss the purpose and suggested methods for doing a case assignment with students. Students may want models of what a well-regarded assignment would be like. Some models may be taken from similar case assignments. The danger in doing so, however, is in generating a formulaic response in which students simply copy the high-grade example. One option is to present several examples.
4. If cases are analyzed in a team, introduce students to resources for team dynamics. The team element alone can cause a lot of frustration for students accustomed to individual assignments. It can burn up time, often creating problems with non-participating students.
5. It may be worthwhile to establish some discussion etiquette guidelines, especially for controversial cases.
6. Allow sufficient class time for students to meet with their teams to discuss the case without necessarily having to schedule a long out-of-class meeting. Some academic thinkers even recommend restricting team meetings to the class period only.
7. Students may benefit from a rough timetable for completing the analysis phase, and clear expectations for the final product. Often groups get stuck on preliminary discussions and lose focus on their objectives.
8. If the case requires students to discuss issues extensively, then an online message board or threaded discussion area may be beneficial. This can allow students to reflect on case issues before providing an answer. The instructor can easily monitor the multiple discussions.
9. Reassure students that the incompleteness of information, deadlines, and the need to make recommendations based on partial analysis are normal both in public service and in life. While that may frustrate them, it is a key learning element of the case method. They should be encouraged to seek the most reasonable solutions given the facts, resources, and circumstances, not the right answer.
10. If you are presenting a case assignment for the first time or piloting a new case, make sure students have an opportunity to provide their reactions and feedback. Student feedback is often invaluable for diagnosing where an assignment may have gone wrong.

Creating Discussion

Generating Debate through Questions

One of the main benefits of the case study approach is that it encourages dialogue and conflict aimed at resolution. Therefore, the opportunity for the teacher is to create a set of opening and leading questions that both elicit response and encourage diverse views. The first question should be simple but open-ended. This helps set the expectation of open-ended answers. Limit the number of questions, and give students enough time to explore each one. Questions encourage participation; if some students are not participating, try directing questions to them. Requiring students to contribute to an online discussion is another way to have the quieter students take part.

As the discussion progresses, follow-up questions can help students to clarify their ideas and be more precise. If students wander off track or introduce irrelevant information, they should be challenged. A question like "What evidence do you have about that from the case?" is a good reality check. Questions can lead students to see their underlying assumptions about how they view case issues. At some point, the teacher might have to impose a process leading beyond analysis and debate. When students are actively participating, the teacher becomes a referee and coach all in one.

Sample Open-Ended Questions

What is happening here?

Who is the decision-maker in the case? What decision is to be made?

What are the decision-maker's objectives?

Are there other important actors? What are their objectives?

What are the key issues? What questions must be addressed or points resolved in order to reach a decision?

What is the environment in which the decision is to be reached? What specific constraints and opportunities will affect the decision?

What specific alternative actions can the decision-maker take? With what consequences?

The case method is a great opportunity for the teacher to practice the Socratic method of inquiry. Of course, as in all teaching, at the same time the teacher is also trying to make sure that all students are engaged, that the learning objectives are being met, that all texting is shut down, and that the discussion reaches a suitable conclusion before the end of class. Therefore, while there is an elegance in the questioning approach, it is constrained by these and other factors.

Signs of a Good Case Discussion

Students and teachers know when case discussions are working for them. It is difficult to assign a metric to this feeling. However, the following are some indicators of a good case discussion:

- How much talking did the instructor do compared with the students?
- How many students were voluntarily active in the discussion?
- How many questions did the instructor ask?
- How many follow-up or challenging questions were asked?
- How energetic was the instructor? What was the level of energy in the discussion?
- Was discussion informed? Was it clear that students had read the case and analyzed it?
- How many high points were there – moments when everyone was engaged, interested, and focused on an issue?
- Did the discussion make sense? Was it coherent?
- Did the discussion conclude with a feeling of satisfactory work done?

Encouraging Problem Solving

It cannot be overemphasized that the objective of a good case is to use complex information, personality, and circumstance to resolve issues in order to learn important lessons. Therefore, the focus has to be on problem solving. But process is also important, because the way in which problems are solved can readily take on great significance. It is a verity of public service that process is important, especially when it involves the rights of citizens, the law, and public service values and ethics. Teaching cases is about managing a process as much or more than it is about getting to the right answer. The way in which problem solving is addressed gives the teacher the opportunity to include process in the ultimate outcome.

What do you really know? Students determining the fact of a case study should be reminded of the fractured, but essentially true statement of former American Secretary of Defense Donald Rumsfeld: "There are known knowns. These are things we know that we know. There are known unknowns. That is to say, there are things that we now know we don't know. But there are also unknown unknowns. These are things we do not know we don't know."

The following are some thoughts on how to evoke a balanced approach to problem solving:

- Encourage students to clearly define the problem first.
- Turn back the quick response with a question such as "How would you do that?"
- Instead of answering questions directly, ask questions of students so they enter into a dialogue about the problem.
- Encourage students to list knowns and unknowns.
- Differentiate between the desired outcome and the specific solutions. This could be described as articulating the strategic goal to be achieved without reference to modalities.
- Ask students what variables a viable solution would take into account. This may help them brainstorm ideas, recognize the presence of secondary issues, and identify high-level sensitivities in the case.
- Encourage students to take a quick break if they are really stuck. Walking or doing something else may "loosen" their thinking.

Jigsaw Cases: One good technique for complex cases involving many dimensions and players or stakeholders is to break a class into groups, each with a distinct part of the problem to work on. They then compare and debate from their various perspectives, often forcing a new synthesis. Complex simulations lend themselves to this process. For more, see http://ublib.buffalo.edu/libraries/projects/cases/teaching/jigsaw.html

To come to a conclusion about a case, or to reach a learning objective, several criteria have to be met. Students must assess and weigh the options; apply relevant theory, especially material taught in class; take into account all pertinent interests, facts, forces, and people; propose a plausible solution; and present their recommendations clearly.

Key Skills to Develop in Students

The case-based approach to learning has proven to be a useful method in developing skills. Key skills that can be embedded into the teaching of case studies include the following:

Group working. The benefits of group working are well documented. Course group work using case studies allows students to share their personal knowledge and experiences, and to deal with conflict and differences of opinion. Care is needed in directing group work (e.g., in selecting group members to ensure smooth group operation, and training students in group-working skills). This is particularly important for longer case studies.

Individual study skills. Case studies are a good vehicle for encouraging students to pursue independent research outside the lecture/tutorial environment.

Information gathering and analysis. Many case studies require resource investigation and encourage students to access a number of different sources, such as the Internet, library, and laboratory results. Sometimes, students are required to interview experts.

Time management. Longer case studies require students to really consider how best to carry out the work so that it is completed on time. Interim meetings with academic staff ensure that students make progress throughout the period of study rather than leaving all the work to the last week.

Presentation skills. Most case studies require students to present their work in a variety of formats; these include oral presentations, PowerPoint presentations, articles, posters, and reports.

Practical skills. Some case studies involve practical work on the components that are being studied.

Things not to do when teaching cases

- Come unprepared to class, without having mastered the facts and details you need to lead the discussion
- Fail to outline a process and stick with it
- Start the discussion with a closed "yes" or "no" question
- Move too quickly to problem definitions or solutions
- Jump to conclusions
- Cut off debate or different perspectives
- Lead students into case presentations or group work unprepared
- Expect all students to respond to cases in the same way
- Fail to draw connections among various student ideas
- Fail to build bridges from one phase to the next

Expanding the Use of Case Studies in Teaching

One consistent theme of this book is that case studies are useful in a variety of learning settings. Their use therefore is not restricted to one methodology. Put more positively, cases present great opportunities both in traditional class settings and in other learning environments.

Adapting Discussion to Class Size

In the classroom setting, the size of the class will dictate what the instructor can do. Small classes permit the whole group to explore a case, whereas large amphitheatre-type classes are not as conducive to the sharing of ideas. In these classes, asking open-ended questions will elicit eager responses from the more outgoing students, but will not draw in or fully engage students who do not speak out in large groups. This does not mean that cases cannot work with large classes; rather, the teaching methodology must suit the situation. For instance, considerable success can be realized by breaking the class into smaller groups. After a discussion period, each group reports to the whole class. Alternatively, the teacher can have the small groups work outside class time and then make a presentation to the class.

Disaggregating Elements of the Case into Groups

Rather than dealing with the whole case, groups can be asked to discuss specific elements and then lead an overall class discussion. One strategy is to assign each step in the case analysis – for example, problem definition, analysis of the environment, review of alternatives, and recommendations – to a different group. In my experience, though, it can be a tricky proposition to divide sequential stages in a case work study because of the dependency between steps. A more effective strategy is to break out the case in sections or stages over a number of classes or learning periods. Different groups can then be assigned a stage to lead on behalf of the entire class. This will take some experience or competency in group leadership from the class.

Alternatively, the work can be divided according to themes. In a case that has multiple elements, such as human relations, conflict, leadership, and problem solving, each group can be asked to look at the case from that perspective.

Building on the Learner's Experience

In teaching cases, and also in their use in organizational learning, consideration has to be given to what experience and academic background students bring to the analysis. Those with little work experience but with good theoretical backgrounds will be more "in the case," using it as the main or sole point of reference to link the real-world problems it poses with theoretical issues. They will have few experiential pointers as terms of reference. However, those with work experience will want to bring that to bear, as will learners within organizations who are using the case for knowledge-building purposes (the search for best practice). Questions such as "How do this case and the lessons learned relate to your own work experience?" can help learners to draw connections between their experience and the case. The challenge for the teacher/facilitator is keeping the discussion on topic. Questions can direct the learner's attention back to the issues raised by the case.

Simulations and Role Playing

Many cases are written as simulated exercises, with detailed scenarios, defined actors, and a problem flow that enables a full class exercise. Other cases present a problem or situation from a number of different perspectives. In the class, groups or individuals can be assigned a role to play or analyze based on such perspectives. These cases are engaging and can enhance class participation.

Voting

In larger groups, students may be asked to vote on decisions, either by a show of hands or electronically using "clicker" technology.[8] This is a good way to engage those who do not speak up in class.

Out-of-Class Assignments

Case analysis does not have to be verbal and in-class. Cases can be used as written assignments just as well. In fact, writing analyses and responses to cases demands that students synthesize a large amount of complex information, distill it into the essence of the issues, and then suggest a means of resolution. Each of these requirements tests a different skill: analysis, synthesis, problem-solving, and communication. Setting the parameters of the assignment can be a challenge for the teacher. Cases at times invite extensive analysis and linkage to the theoretical teaching of the course. At other times, the requirement is not for detailed analytical work but for a concise synthesis of the analysis – saying more with fewer words. Some of the features of a written assignment that the teacher might want to look for are precision in analysis; effective problem definition; review of alternatives; analysis of risks, opportunities, and key variables; and a plausible course of action or decision framework for moving forward.

Distance Education

The case study method of teaching permits considerable interpretation and discussion among students and between students and teacher. This interaction need not be restricted to the physical classroom. As social networking media proliferate, the capacity to share commentary and manage discussions increases. Cases are increasingly being used in distance education. However, to use them successfully requires considerable planning and time on the part of the instructor. As well, there are challenges in monitoring and steering these much more freewheeling discussions.

Using Real-Life Cases in the Classroom

More will be said about organizational learning cases in Chapter 5. However, such cases can readily be used in the classroom context and linked to theory. One of the objectives of a real-life case is to identify lessons learned from the experience. Often, these lessons are reported in the case itself, in some form of evaluation. However, the teacher will also want to embellish this with the observations and contributions of students. In other words, while there may be obvious formal lessons learned, what lessons do the students observe?

One of the challenges of using real-life cases in a classroom setting is that the outcome may be known. Therefore, the objective of finding a solution may be somewhat constrained. Yet students can still propose and evaluate alternative courses of action. Real-life cases often have dramatic elements whose currency makes their discussion inherently interesting.

A further challenge in teaching real-life cases is to find the bridge between that experience – the case – and the experience of the students, focusing on such questions as

- What are the key lessons of this case that may have some application in your future work environment?
- Could this situation or challenge happen to you?
- Do you see yourself in this situation or one like it?
- Were there successful practices in this case that might be of use to you?

Grading Case Study Analyses

In the classroom, grading systems vary and follow the practice of the institution and the preference of the instructor. Grading case work is more challenging because it is not undertaken only in written form. Teachers have to take into account full class discussions as well as the results of group work. Standards need to be set in place in advance. The following are some suggestions of issues to be taken into account when applying the established grading methodology:

1. Does the student adequately understand the facts in the case?
2. Did the student read the case carefully enough to identify the important aspects of the organization's internal and external circumstances?
3. Are the strengths and weaknesses identified consistent with the organization's mission, the facts presented, and the dynamics at play?
4. Has the student dealt adequately with the constraints and opportunities facing decision-makers?
5. Is the analysis deep enough? Does it go into sufficient depth to identify and deal with the critical underlying issues?
6. Has the student used theories and concepts from this (and other) classes in making the analysis?

7. Is the student trying to get by on intuition and common sense alone or did he or she use theories, research, and concepts from the management literature to deepen the analysis?
8. Has the student used the information in the case creatively? Does the analysis hold together?
9. Has the student integrated different pieces of information in the case to come up with new insights into the situation, or did the student merely followed a formula and repeat what was already stated in the case?
10. Are the recommendations feasible given the student's assumptions?
11. Did the student organize his or her report well and is it internally consistent?
12. Has the student presented his or her analysis and recommendations in a literate and effective manner? Is the report or presentation well written and does it communicate clearly; is it free of unnecessary jargon and obfuscation?

Notes

[1] J. R. Feagin, A. Orum, and G. Sjoberg, eds., *A Case for the Case Study* (Chapel Hill, NC: University of North Carolina Press, 1991).

[2] R. Heitzman, "Case Study Instruction in Teacher Education: Opportunity to Develop Students' Critical Thinking, School Smarts and Decision Making," *Education* (Summer 2008), 1.

[3] *Writing Case Studies: A Manual*, abridged version adapted for use by the Online Learning Centre, http://olc.spsd.sk.ca/de/pd/instr/strats/casestd/casestds.pdf.

[4] B. Duch, "Problems: A Key Factor in PBL" (Center for Teaching Effectiveness, University of Delaware, 1997), http://www.udel.edu/pbl/cte/spr96-phys.html.

[5] B. Duch, "Characteristics of Good Problems" (Center for Teaching Effectiveness, University of Delaware, 1997), point 4, http://www.udel.edu/pbl/cte/spr96-phys.html.

[6] Ibid.

[7] P.R. Lawrence, "The Preparation of Case Material," in *The Case Method of Teaching Human Relations and Administration*, ed. K.R. Andrews (Cambridge, MA: Harvard University Press, 1953), 215.

[8] D. Duncan, *Clickers in the Classroom: How to Enhance Science Teaching Using Classroom Response Systems* (Pearson Education, 2005).

Chapter 4

A User's Guide: Case Studies from the Learner's Perspective

> *A case is a text that refuses to explain itself.*
>
> – W. Ellet

No discussion of the case study methodology would be complete without considering the perspective of the learner or user of cases. Just as teachers need a different set of strategies for case studies than they do for lectures, so too students or users – the other partner in the relationship – need to approach cases somewhat differently from other learning and testing tools. In the context of organizational learning or knowledge transfer, the reader or user of a case study needs to view the case not simply as a story of general interest but as a mine of information and insight that might be of use or applicability in his or her own situation. Getting to that rich vein involves taking certain approaches.

There is certainly some mythology around the use of case studies in any form of education. While this methodology is typical of law, medical, and business schools, the use of case studies in public administration education (both formal academic training and organizational training within governments) is limited. That is changing, for the better. However, what must be overcome is the idea that the case study methodology demands some mysterious set of skills. It does have its challenges, but they can be overcome and to good effect.

In Chapter 3, I explained that the case study method requires students to learn in ways that may be unfamiliar to them. They are invited to be active participants in analyzing problems and recommending solutions. But many students lack experience with an open-ended, problem-solving format in the classroom. Students who view education as mastering a set of well-defined facts may be uncomfortable with the ambiguity inherent in case studies. Students often want to know the right answer, but case studies replicate a real-world context where there can be many right answers. Further, case studies demand that students make decisions based on incomplete information, where important facts are missing. It can be a challenge for students to analyze these situations, define the issues, apply a theoretical perspective, and research and propose a course of action or alternatives.

This chapter expands on a handbook that I developed for graduate students at the School of Policy Studies, Queen's University. Some students were encountering the case study approach for the first time and were uncertain about what was expected of them. The handbook explains what case studies are, how they are used in the classroom, and what methods students can employ in their analyses, group work, and presentations. The first two topics are mentioned only briefly here, as they are covered in some depth in the previous chapters. This chapter focuses on some approaches to help learners in the process of working through case studies.

What Is Expected of Students?

In assigning case studies in public administration, instructors expect students to study and understand the information provided in the case, diagnose the nature of the problem, set the problem within the context of relevant public policy and management theory, research alternate ways to resolve the problem, and recommend and justify a course of action.

What's in it for the student? By preparing solutions to cases studies, students will be exposed to a variety of policy and management situations. Their decision-making skills will be enhanced as they sift through large volumes of information to identify problems, determine goals, evaluate alternatives, and develop plans to implement decisions. They will hone their ability to apply analytical tools in true-to-life public policy and administration situations. By preparing reports, they will learn how to express themselves succinctly, both orally and in writing. By working in groups or presenting ideas and solutions in class, they will also develop the ability to defend the logic of their analysis and conclusions. These are all valuable skills for a future public service leader.

Case studies, whether fictional or factual, pose serious policy and managerial dilemmas – the kinds of challenges faced by actors in the public sector on a day-to-day basis. Case studies challenge students to take into account all the variables that might have a bearing on the situation. Often the goal is to find a feasible solution that balances competing interests and needs. In cases that are factual and for which the outcome is known, the exercise is not to arrive at the known conclusion, but to use the information to form an argued view on the outcome and also to derive from what is presented what alternative courses of action might have been possible, and what can be learned and applied to other situations.

Students can feel overwhelmed by the information or complexity of a case when they first read it. In order to derive the most from the use of case studies, a phased approach is recommended.

Phases of Case Study Review

Regardless of the length or complexity of a case, students typically work through a number of steps or phases to analyze the case study, develop a working hypothesis, evaluate alternatives, and propose a course of action:

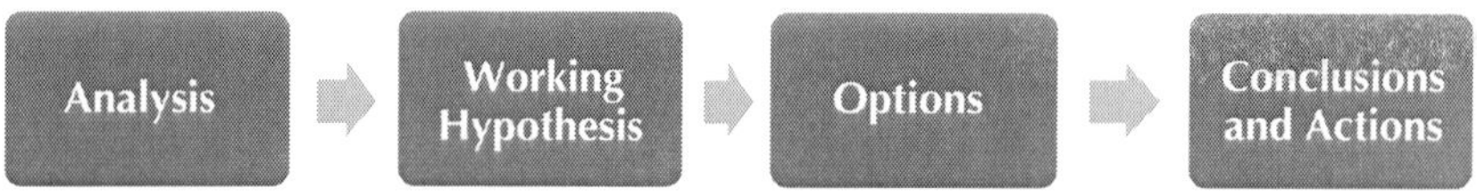

Analytical Phase

Good cases involve a mix of linear facts and context, and softer information about people, history, and culture. The analysis is therefore rich and varied. Students are challenged to answer a number of questions, for example,

- What exactly is going on here?
- What are the underlying issues at play?
- What do the events or circumstances mean in the context of the area we are studying or the questions being asked?
- What in this case is of primary importance and what is background?
- Who are the key players? What did they do?
- What issues arise as a result of what they did or did not do?
- What policy and administrative constraints, expectations, and issues can be identified?

To begin to the process of analysis, I suggest that students read the case several times without trying to answer questions or solve problems. The aim is to identify and understand the policy or managerial problem being described. If students are working in groups, phrases such as "What I see going on here is..." should predominate. Students may think that they comprehend the problem and that the answer is obvious, but they should avoid jumping to conclusions at this stage.

Study the assignment questions and review the learning objectives. This will determine how to go about the work of applying theory and arriving at a solution. Often case study assignments will ask students to adopt a certain approach or address specific questions. Ignore these at your peril.

Start to define the salient issues, and make note of these. In complex cases, it can be helpful to use charts or "issue maps" to brainstorm and record ideas. Bear in mind that cases, like real-world situations, may contain information of little importance to the main problem. The analysis should take all the facts into account, but differentiate between what is important and what is not. Look for the "elephants in the room" – the big issues that might not be articulated by the actors, the implicit assumptions or prejudices that need to recognized and addressed.

Consider the points of view inherent in the case. The case might be presented through the eyes of a central character, but that does not preclude other perspectives. Avoid picking "good guys" and "bad guys"; quick value judgments often lead to narrow and unhelpful perspectives.

Decide which principles, theories, or models can be applied to the case and the assigned task. Theoretical material is to be used in the analysis and solution of problems, not as an afterthought.

The Working Hypothesis

Students can easily get stuck in the analysis stage. So-called paralysis by analysis is a hazard of the case study method because the information students have to work with is often incomplete. Students must be prepared, perhaps after a set period of time, to move on despite the missing pieces. As the Grayson Walker Teaching Resource Centre of the University of Tennessee points out in its guidelines for using cases, this means that teachers/facilitators should "not let the discussion get submerged in the details of the case, but rather ensure that discussion focuses on the ways to solve the problem."[1]

As tempting as it might be, students should avoid proposing a solution that is so sweeping or unrealistic that it cannot lead to a plausible course of action. For example, recommending that the Constitution be amended in the next few months will not move the case forward. Likewise, proposing that leaders be dismissed for incompetence might be satisfying, but is not likely to happen in the real world. Vague generalities need to be avoided. Specific behaviours need to be identified.

Now is the time for students to articulate their inferences and judgments about the case. These inferences should be supported with evidence. For example, if students infer that conflict exists among certain actors, they should be able to justify this interpretation with evidence from the case. Other students might disagree. Creative conflict should be encouraged. An advantage to working in groups is that students bring different

> *Working in groups* is a very useful approach to working through cases. Each individual will see the situation from a different perspective or take a unique approach. Group discussions will help surface these different points of view so that students can take advantage of alternative perspectives.

viewpoints. Solutions that account for these differences will be more balanced.

A working hypothesis describes the problem and proposes some solutions. The following questions can help students to develop a working hypothesis.

- What courses of action or inaction are possible in this situation?
- For factual cases, what alternative courses of action might have been inferred, even though the one taken is known?
- What are the risks of the various actions? What is the risk intensity and impact?
- What is the risk of inaction?

Evaluating Options

In this phase, students assess their options; they "evaluate the strengths, weaknesses, opportunities, and threats to each course of action."[2] In doing so, students should consider such questions as

- Who will be affected by each course of action? Who wins and who loses?
- What has to change in order to achieve an option? What practices have to change? What policies?
- What are the risks of each option?
- Is there quantitative evidence in support of any options?
- What principal values are at play that must guide the conclusion? Legal, moral, ethical, regard for people, fairness, equity?
- What are the most important criteria in coming to a final course of action? Public values? Policy requirements? Re-establishing control of a situation? The need to sustain the organization? The need to change the organization?
- Are there time sequences for the options? How long will they take? Can actions be deferred? What needs to be done quickly?

Conclusions and Action

Based on the preceding analysis – the stages of problem definition, theoretical underpinning, options and evaluation – students must now "make a decision regarding a satisfactory or at least workable plan of action."[3] The decision should reflect the overriding themes of the analysis and the values most relevant to the case. Students may wish to refer to their "issue map" to make sure that their solution addresses the salient issues.

The solution should have a ring of authenticity and "do-ability" to it. It should be possible to implement in a realistic time frame and sequence of activity. Things cannot all happen at once. People cannot be in several places at once. Organizations cannot accommodate all the changes desired in the wink of an eye. Students should identify the actors who must take the actions, establish the desired outcomes, and state the criteria for evaluating the outcomes.

In some cases, process can be an answer. When the information is incomplete, further consultation is needed with stakeholders, and resources have not been marshaled to implement the course of action, the most appropriate option might be to study the situation more or to defer a decision. However, students should not resort to the "more information syndrome" without good cause.

The sequence of phases outlined here might seem like a lot of work. In fact, this sequential approach becomes fluid and interactive as students acquire greater facility with cases. The steps are intended to provide some structure for students unfamiliar with case analysis, and to serve as a checklist for students who may be more experienced with this approach.

Case Presentations

Communicating case findings effectively requires more than merely telling an audience the steps you went through in your analysis. It will involve a structured argument to convince your audience that you have correctly identified the problem, linked it to broader circumstances, examined alternatives, and proposed an appropriate course of action. For cases that are oriented toward knowledge sharing, it will involve outlining the lessons learned from the case and assessing how transferable they are.

The format of a case presentation will depend on what is asked of the students, whether they worked in groups or individually, and whether the presentation is delivered orally or in writing. A successful presentation, regardless of its form, will offer a thoughtful analysis and set of responses.

Written Reports

The key to a well-written report is a sound structure and a concise narrative. The report should summarize the results of your thinking, rather than taking readers on a winding journey. The student is wise to follow a simple structure of summary, problem analysis, environmental analysis, options, and suggested course of action.

Group Presentations

Students are often asked to work in groups outside of class time to prepare an in-depth analysis of a case and then present their solution to the class as a whole. In some instances, they are asked to lead a class discussion. These are two different kinds of work and so clarity is needed about what is expected. For the latter, the groups have two tasks: analyze the case and develop a set of questions for leading class discussion. Group members have to decide who will lead the discussion, or assign roles to different group members such as opener, questioner(s), and concluder. For the former, the group will have to undertake a full cycle of case review. Groups will want to summarize their review and use an accessible format such as PowerPoint to present their findings to the class.

What to Avoid in Any Case Presentation

Repeating the case: Summarize the case and point out the most important issues, but do not retell it as a time filler.

Paralysis by analysis: Good analysis is important, but it is only the start of a case presentation. Balance the amount of analysis with options, environmental risks and opportunities, proposed responses, and implementation.

Jumping to conclusions: A case presentation is an argument for a set of conclusions or solutions to problems presented. Case studies are used to build thinking processes in complex environments rich with human interaction. A successful presentation leads the reader or audience to a set of conclusions. It does not push them.

Time travelling: The solutions presented should reflect a realistic time frame. For instance, organizational cultures do not change overnight, but the process of changing them can be started.

Clichéd responses: When addressing issues, be sufficiently rich in detail to indicate you understand what you are proposing and not simply dropping in an idea because it is part of the usual mix of solutions. For instance, if there are communication problems in the situation, simply saying you will have a communications plan tells the reader nothing about that plan, how it will be carried out, and what it aims to accomplish.

Notes

[1] Grayson H. Walker Teaching Resource Center, University of Tennessee, "Underlying Procedures for Using Cases," http://www.utc.edu/Administration/WalkerTeachingResourceCenter/FacultyDevelopment/CaseTeaching/index.html.

[2] Ibid.

[3] Ibid.

CHAPTER 5

SHARING EXPERIENCE: USING CASE STUDIES FOR ORGANIZATIONAL LEARNING

Don't find a fault, find a remedy.
– Henry Ford

Case studies have always been used beyond classroom pedagogy, as important as that is. Increasingly, they are proving to be valuable tools in the creation and transfer of knowledge within public sector organizations. To see their value and use in this context, it is necessary to understand how knowledge management works within public organizations. Although the idea of knowledge management has been around for many decades, recent changes in technology such as social networking and communities of practice linking practitioners across diverse organizations have increased the need for more knowledge management and facilitated its implementation.

The Link to Knowledge Management

The sharing of experience and knowledge within organizations has always been a challenge. There is a frequently cited criticism that organizations, especially public ones, fail to adequately learn from their mistakes. It can equally be argued that, given the rush of events and speedy transmission of information that is normal today, these same organizations also fail to take the time to learn from their successes. Everyone is rushed. People move on and forget the new ideas that worked to solve a problem or ease a process. While in the public sector, major events may lead to official enquiries that determine fault or, on a rare basis, distribute praise, the completion of a project successfully, the adaptation to new service practices, and the conversion of systems and organizations to meet new challenges are seldom documented.[1]

Making the Case: Using Case Studies for Teaching and Knowledge Management in Public Administration, A. Graham. Montreal and Kingston: McGill-Queen's University Press, Queen's Policy Studies Series.

A 2008 report to the Brazilian Chamber of Deputies summarizes the need for some form of knowledge management:

> To preserve this knowledge base is a fundamental necessity lest we run into an eternal cycle of new beginnings and remain forever in the need of consolidating best practices. To avoid this, mechanisms have to be generated and instituted permitting new initiatives to become the support to new proposals so that experience can produce shortcuts and render effectiveness to governmental actions.[2]

This problem is not simply associated with administrative challenges of day-to-day management. Governments around the world are continually designing, implementing, and adapting policies. They are managing complex situations that occasionally arise from natural disasters, major systemic failures, and the confrontation of competing demands and forces. How they manage these to greater or lesser success can be a matter of significance to many citizens. The techniques used, experiences gained, and solutions developed can also be of use to other public sector practitioners. However, in the onslaught of events and scarcity of resources, governments often fail to learn from their past experiences in a systematic way.

> *Good judgment comes from experience. Experience comes from bad judgment.*
>
> – Walter Wriston, former CEO of Citibank
>
> The greatest value-added in the use of case studies in professional training is not the accumulation of facts but the growth of judgment. Walter Wriston argues that good judgment cannot be taught; it can only grow through experience. Thus, professional training should have a significant *experiential* dimension. Book learning is not enough. Case studies can meet this need.

For several decades there has been a growing interest in what is termed knowledge management, generally defined as the ways in which an organization organizes, retains, and distributes its accumulated knowledge. It is widely recognized that public sector organizations deal primarily with knowledge and that most public servants are considered as knowledge workers. Further, this dependence upon accumulated information within an organization that is transformed into relevant knowledge is spreading to public service professions that have previously been seen as more hands-on. For instance, most police services now have computers in their vehicles, requiring instant data entry about an incident but also equipping front-line officers with complete information on the individuals they encounter, the area in which they are working, and related crimes.

Where do case studies fit into building organizational knowledge? When addressing this question, it is useful to set the flow of information and creation of knowledge into a context. The pyramid illustrates how data, when organized and shared, evolves toward both knowledge and wisdom:

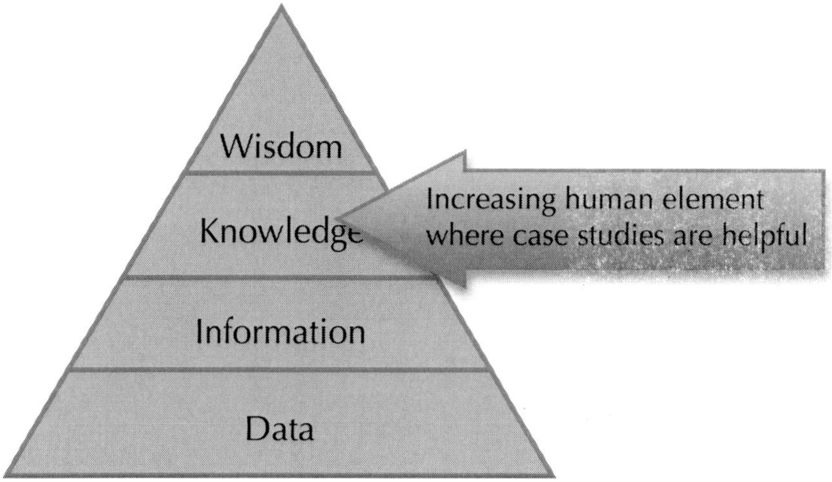

Case studies in the organizational context play a useful role in the presentation of tacit knowledge. Tacit knowledge is often characterized as the know-how within an organization, in comparison – or, more correctly, in companionship – with know-what. Tacit knowledge has certain characteristics that are linked to the use of cases, either formally or informally: Tacit knowledge is acquired primarily through experience, it is not easily put into words and passed on others, and it is most effectively communicated one-to-one or through stories.

The objective of using case studies in organizational knowledge management is to convey to the user both the actual activities undertaken to meet a specific challenge (the what) and the means taken (the how) with a full portrayal of the context. Case studies are designed to provide a sharing of learned experiences within organizations, across organizations, among colleagues, and across generations. That being said, case studies occupy a beneficial but unique position in knowledge management or, as characterized here, organizational learning. For instance, case studies, by their very nature, focus on a given situation, set of facts, or events. They therefore do not present all the accumulated knowledge of an organization in a systematic fashion. That is the role of information retention systems, formal evaluations and studies, and the increasingly large databases maintained by public organizations.

Batista and colleagues,[3] in their 2005 study, suggest that knowledge management applies to government agencies in the following way:

FIGURE 5.1
A Schematic of Knowledge Management Tools

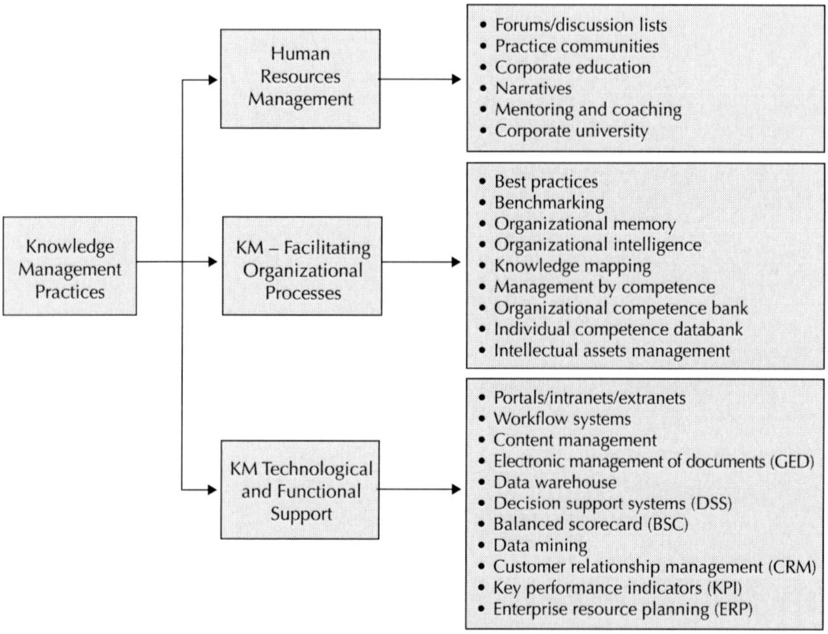

Reprinted by permission from F. F. Batista et al., "Gestão do Conhecimento na Administração Pública" [Knowledge Management in Public Administration] (Brasilia: IPEA, 2005), p. 26.

Case studies within the organizational learning context highlight specific events or projects, give them a richer context, and identify the learning elements potentially relevant to other people or organizations. As we will see below, people rely as much on stories and experience as they do on information objectively presented. Further, by doing things within an organization, people discover what works, what does not work, or how a novel idea can improve productivity or alleviate a particularly challenging situation. While these techniques and findings do not always translate well in other circumstances, they can. Case studies provide a way to document such learning. They give the reader or user some sense of how these approaches worked or did not work, providing cautionary tales as well as potentially useful insights for action.

Storytelling as Informal Organizational Learning

The informal transfer of knowledge (know-what) and experience (know-how) is a continuous process within any organization. In truth, there is no substitute for this informal exchange. It takes place at a human level. It derives its power from storytelling and experience sharing. This is a rich way to learn, as storytelling provides information not just about what happened and what was done, but also about why certain actions took place, who played what role, and how they achieved what they did. Stories provide a richness of context that is a challenge to document in more traditional, linear styles of reporting.

Informal organizational learning will always be found when people gather together in any way, but from a knowledge management perspective, it suffers from certain inadequacies. It is sporadic in that some hear of the experience while others do not. There is no assurance that the stories will reach all who would benefit from the knowledge they impart, because the knowledge is not distributed in a systematic fashion. Moreover, informality of exchange is not sustainable in that the teller of the story may move on and the knowledge get lost.

Some of the questions a practitioner will ask when reviewing a case study:

- How did that work?
- What should I avoid?
- What can I apply?
- Will this help me improve my practice?

Informal storytelling and sharing of experience is seldom contestable in the way that more formally available information is. By this is meant that, while the story and sharing can be rich and beneficial in a specific context, public organizations seldom face situations where solutions are clearly drawn, processes work at peak efficiency, and judgment and understanding are exact and immutable. Conversational storytelling, as useful as it is in the moment, does not provide for debate and systematic review of alternatives and, perhaps most importantly, the application of this knowledge to a different circumstance.

This is not to detract from the great value that can be derived from hearing from those involved in situations or challenges from which others can learn. In addition, the presence of the key person who made the decision or assessed a situation is a rare opportunity to draw not just from "the what" of their experience but also to understand the more nuanced why and how. The challenge becomes how to share it widely and in a systematic fashion where that is needed.

The Search for New Organizational Learning Tools

For this reason, public organizations – in fact, all organizations – are increasingly looking for more systematic ways to build organizational learning. They are looking for ways to share experience, both good and bad, while avoiding onerous processes of review that can be readily politicized or excessively judgmental, especially at the personal level.

Governments are increasingly trying to take a systematic approach to organizational learning. Some have adopted special incentive programs for the creation of case studies to share experience. Their application can be systematic, used in formal teaching settings, or equally available to practitioners and the interested public for general use. A good example is the ANZSOG Case Program, create by the Australia and New Zealand School of Government. Cases are used extensively within the formal training program of the school. The incentive programs provide funds for academics or practitioners to write cases for that application.[4]

> **What an organizational case study is not:** "It is important also to describe what a case study is not. It's not a story intended either to validate or denigrate someone's career, project, or mission. That is, it does not set out to illustrate per se the good or the bad (or the ugly), but is designed to teach by telling a story in an objective, usually third-person narrative. Using the story, the reader can draw conclusions and learn lessons through contextual or experience-based learning. We are not so interested in second-guessing decisions but rather in thinking through how decisions are made."
>
> – Ed Rodgers, Chief Knowledge Officer, Godard Space Flight Centre, NASA, 2008.

How can organizations benefit more fully from the rich oral tradition of storytelling and marry that up with the broader application of systematic case studies? Aside from the example above, there are a number of ways now being used or considered. YouTube provides a simple means of converting a story told face-to-face to one that is recorded and distributed widely. Further, organizations can sponsor the creation of case studies on issues that they have faced and from which they want to ensure some lessons are noted and passed on. Organizations can have the best of both worlds if they tap the experience of their longer serving employees. Many organizations have centralized training programs to bring together those who have dealt with challenging issues and those who would benefit from that experience. At these sessions, employees interact with a key player and participate in a facilitated discussion of the case. There is nothing richer than this combination.

A Continuum of Cases for Teaching and Organizational Learning

Fine distinctions are difficult to draw between formal teaching cases and those that we are calling organizational learning cases. In fact, the latter can well form the basis for the former. However, it is both timely and useful to have such a distinction. The motivation for doing so is to encourage organizations to develop learning strategies that adapt cases as a tool that is not restricted to formal educational objectives.

Teaching cases are powerful instruments not only in formal educational institutions but also in organizations. Many teaching cases are based on fact sets and the experiences of public organizations. Teaching cases can also be fictional, created in such a way to draw out a particular theory or to test a set of assumptions. Whether factual or fictional, teaching cases are designed to meet specific teaching objectives. The scope of analysis, while it can be complex and demanding, is limited to those objectives.

> *In dialogue, people become observers of their own thinking.*
> – Peter Senge
>
> Organizations that perform well and show resilience in this dynamic world are organizations that *learn*. The capacity to learn depends on the ability of an organization to have a *dialogue* within itself, because it is through dialogue that thinking is critically re-evaluated. The case method of organizational learning models dialogue, and builds the skills of participants to practice it.

Organizational learning cases, on the other hand, are fact-based. The aim is to share information, richly presented with ample context, for decision-makers and actors within organizations to use and adapt to their own challenges. Organizational learning cases are intended to transfer knowledge – be it technique, lore, or a deep understanding of how an issue was managed – to those who may lack the experience or awareness of a situation. The learning comes from the actions taken, the lessons learned, and the practices identified as successful or not.

Can the same case be used for both formal teaching and organizational learning? Certainly it can. As well, it can be argued that there is a continuum between formal teaching and organizational learning. Like so much in public sector management and policy, the lines of distinction are blurred. Figure 5.3 illustrates how teaching and organizational learning cases are related.

FIGURE 5.2
The Interaction of Teaching Cases and Organizational Learning

Formal Teaching Cases – Theory Driven	Teaching Cases: Methods and Objectives	Organizational Learning	Organizational Learning – Deeper Understanding
• Analysis • Connection to theory	• Action learning • Simulations • Decision-making • Skills learning	• Lessons learned • Skills shared • Practical tips	• Intensive documentation • Layers of understanding • Develops a complete picture

Case Studies as a Strategic Organizational Tool

Organizational learning cases have a strategic intent, with learning at its core. These cases therefore become a strategic tool in an organization's knowledge management strategy, and an active element in how organizations manage sustainability challenges. Sustainability in this context refers to the ability of an organization to retain its key cultural and operational values over time while adapting to changing circumstances. Organizational learning cases are becoming part of the memory bank of the organization, a way to formally tell the stories that are so important to sustaining values and culture, and a sense of achievement that reinforces future action.

Some of the goals of organizational case studies are to

- Create a complete record of a complex challenge so that those interested develop a full understanding of context, response, rationale, and repercussions
- Tell the story to significant publics
- Share the thinking and context behind the actions taken
- Celebrate success and document failure in a way that permits an understanding of the factors salient to each
- Identify practices that were innovative or exemplary to solving similar problems
- Provide cautionary advice either within the organization or to the broader professional environment about dangers or steps best avoided
- Support the organization's effort to gain long-term support, be that in the form of additional resources, internal alignment and recognition, or public confidence

The key test of a good organizational learning case is: What works for whom in what circumstances?

Avoiding the Dead End of Self-Congratulation

There is an important distinction between an organizational learning case and an advertisement. It does not take much of an Internet search for organizational case studies to land on the site of a consulting firm that lists a series of "case studies." These tend to be brief descriptions of consulting projects that did not merely go well but performed organizational turnarounds of near miraculous proportions. Lessons learned, if there are any, consist for the most part in praise for the consulting firm, the client wise enough to choose it, and the leaders all round for their wisdom and foresight.

An organizational learning case has to be useful, credible, and complete. Governments and public agencies are continually performing at exceptional levels on many fronts. These achievements need to be documented and shared, along with the failures. But the successes and failures are seldom clear-cut. In most cases we encounter a zone of complexity, often characterized as the great muddling through. Some things went well, and some did not.

The key objective of the organizational case study is to transfer knowledge in all its forms for possible application elsewhere. In the real world of public sector practice, that means the good, the bad, and the ambiguous. Once again, apply the test: What works for whom, and in what circumstances? Organizations should not set out to document only their crowning achievements. Even when they do, the sharing of information requires a considerable degree of humility and modesty of presentation. There is something inherent in the public sector culture that would encourage that.

Here are a number of steps that will help insulate the writers of case studies from accusations of self-congratulations or displays of organizational ego:

1. Clearly state the goals of the case in terms of lessons learned, valuable insights, and transferable knowledge.
2. Use information and assessments from parties external to the organization, such as formal audits and reports, third-party commentary, and academic writing.
3. Avoid creating heroes and villains; in practice, there are few of either type.
4. Be realistic about results, in terms of both expectations and actual outputs or outcomes.
5. Do not declare a project a success if it is still underway.
6. The more assertive the statements of success or failure, the clearer the evidence should be.

A balanced presentation is especially important in the communication and documentation of how risk was managed. Risk, the anticipation of outcomes or events that will materially affect the key objectives of an organization or program, can be understood only in the context in which the risks were recognized and mitigated. Further, the mitigation, be it risk acceptance or avoidance, can be understood only when all other factors and actions around the risk decision are fully understood. A case study provides that detail.

No case, therefore, can be presented as a total success or total failure. There is complexity and something to learn from how success was achieved, how risk was managed, what worked and what did not and, perhaps most importantly, how the organization adapted as it learned and experimented.

Areas That Lend Themselves to Organizational Case Studies

The spectrum of public sector activity is vast. There is always something to learn or some practical tip or lesson to share within and across organizations. However, some areas lend themselves to organizational case studies.

Major Projects

Governments undertake all kinds of projects within their ongoing operating environments. Some projects are very large, for example, a major road construction project. Some are small, such as the implementation of new routines by a task group. Projects and project management issues lend themselves to case studies for a number of reasons. In general, projects have a discrete time horizon: they begin and they end. This permits the preparation of a case that can tell a more complete story, which is harder to do for ongoing government programs. The goals of the project are defined, to varying degrees of clarity. While the question "Did the project achieve what it set out to do?" may not be easy to answer, there is at least a starting point for analysis. The skills demanded in project management tend to be different than those of normal program management, and they are transferable from one project to another. Therefore, there is much to learn from a project in terms of knowledge transfer.

Major Policy Change and Implementation

This area has to be a major focus of knowledge development and transfer in government. Much time and higher level academic education is devoted to the creation of public policy. So, too, is much political time and attention. Considerably less is aimed at understanding how policies are implemented and then instilling that understanding in those responsible for the rollout of new policy or the adjustment of existing ones. However, the realization of public policy objectives is at the heart of the enterprise. One concern in creating case studies is that they can draw attention to highly political and contentious issues, and this will be discussed more in the next section. The principal point here is that increasingly governments need to build on their policy experiences, learn from them, and transfer what is learned to inform future efforts.

Emergency Response Situations

The range of emergency response within the public sector seems limitless. As public organizations adopt a more resilience-oriented approach to perceived risks (a pandemic) and to anticipated disasters (hurricanes, fires), they are also developing a body of knowledge about responses. Emergency response generally has internal requirements for record keeping and post-incident reporting and evaluation. Major incidents almost inevitably lead to investigations of what happened, what went wrong and, to a lesser degree, what went right. It could be argued that emergency responses are so thoroughly documented that case studies have little to offer. In terms of investigating the incident, this is probably true. However, case studies are invaluable as a means of transferring this knowledge from one specialized area to another.

The objective of the case study is not to find fault or to present a detailed picture for future policy-making or response adjustment. It is to document practices within the response from which others can learn, and to provoke a discussion of options that might have been pursued by the actors in the situation.

Extraordinary Response Situations

Similar to an emergency response, these are situations in which organizations have to mount major efforts to deal with surges in demand, rapidly changing circumstances, or the failure to respond earlier. Unlike organizations that are emergency-oriented, most public organizations have normal, day-to-day operating conditions. When those conditions change, the organizational response can often test the organization's capacity. How organizations respond is of great interest. It usually entails some extraordinary efforts in organizational leadership, teamwork, and systems capacity to manage a highly pressurized political demand to "clean up the mess."

> *Don't find fault. Find a remedy.*
> – Henry Ford
>
> Case studies and discussions of them will generally deal with mistakes that were made. The point of the discussion should not be to keep score of these errors, but to find practical solutions to problems. It is easy to criticize someone else's thinking, but it is much harder to present your own original solutions. Perhaps the greatest challenge for practitioners is to see what in that case and those errors they can use to improve their own organization before the same mistake gets made – on their turf.

Organizational Changes

Few topics elicit more concern and stress than organizational change. This can range from internal changes to major departmental or agency shifts. While each change is unique, each also has elements common to the organizational change process. One reason that cases are so useful in this area is that public managers make organizational changes on a sporadic basis and see each change as special. Because such changes are not part of the normal routine, managers do not draw lines of comparison. They seldom ask how it was done in this or that organization, even though there is a rich history of organizational change. Cases lend themselves to being of real value in this area.

Innovative Practice

Governments and public managers are constantly innovating on a number of fronts: new policies, new models of governance, new organizational models, new solutions in terms of technology and delivery, and new ways to solve immediate challenges. There is much to learn from the experience of others, and not only in a cautionary sense. Of course, the mistakes of others and how they responded provide very useful information. However, case studies of innovative practice with good information on what worked and what did not enable governments and their organizations to consider options that might not have been on their agenda.

Dealing with Politically Sensitive Issues

In the public sector, the potential for creating political embarrassment is a very real and pressing impediment to full and frank disclosure of experiences that may be of benefit to others. Political leaders and public servants tend toward a high level of risk aversion, sometimes to the point of accepting the risk of concealing or avoiding the full release of information. Case studies could be readily perceived as a risk. And they can be, if they are poorly written. However, the risk of pointing to error has to be balanced with the risk of repeating it – having ignored the signposts of what not to do.

That being said, there are some real concerns with the pursuit of case studies in government. There is the danger of some piece of information emerging from a case that will prompt a question in the legislature, media attention, or even political scandal. This danger remains long after the incident occurred. In addition, some piece of information now in the public domain but somehow not noticed the first time may attract media or public attention. The case study may be written in such a way that the facts, albeit already known, appear to reveal something new, leading to a media spiral of how this information was withheld in the first place. Such problems occur at random and are difficult to avoid.

None of this should deter the use of case studies in the public sector. What it should do is encourage a prudent approach to politically sensitive areas. Most governments today have some form of privacy legislation guiding their use of information. Because cases often involve individual decision and behaviour, considerable care has to be taken to protect the privacy rights of all involved. Using information in the public domain, and obtaining permission to quote interviews and personal communications, are good practices. In addition, I recommend the following:

- Avoid creating case studies for policy areas or projects that are not complete. If a case study is based on an ongoing practice, every effort should be made to define an end point for the case itself.
- Anticipate that these cases will be public documents in one form or another.
- Document sources and avoid hearsay.
- Avoid extrapolations or conclusions that appear editorial. Leave that to the reader.

- Create a distance between the case and its writer. Use a third-person narrator.
- Have the case thoroughly reviewed by an arm's-length source.
- Ideally the case study should not be published or distributed by the organization that is the subject of the case. This can be seen as self-serving.

Embedding the Use of Case Studies into Organizational Culture

Case studies can be used wherever existing knowledge can contribute to future action within an organization. Their existence, in whatever form, is not simply for heuristic or general interest purposes. They play a much more significant role than staff training, as important as that is. Some organizations, as part of their deeply embedded culture, place a great value on finding ways to learn from their experiences, holding that experience up to scrutiny and improving their operations as a result.

> Cases studies are useless unless they answer the question "So what?" for the busy practitioner.

The following anecdote illustrates how learning from the experience of others can inform good practice:

> A good example of how case studies are used in design comes from John Roebling's design of the Brooklyn Bridge in New York City. Civil engineers in the 19th century lacked the necessary aerodynamic knowledge to properly model suspension bridges. After studying multiple bridge collapses, Roebling decided that the only logical approach was to make the bridge as tough as possible. These formed important case studies for the engineer. Roebling built the bridge to handle six times the stresses he expected it would accommodate in even the worst situations. During the bridge's design, he placed extensive restrictions on the number of people allowed to stand on the bridge, their movement patterns, and other factors. When asked why he was convinced that the bridge would stand, Roebling would always point out just how strong he was building the bridge, and exactly why it was so strong. While it might appear that this kind of caution is obvious, it should be noted that Roebling's bridge is one of the few examples of 19th century suspension bridges still standing. All of the bridges built by his contemporaries have collapsed.[5]

Such an anecdote may itself be a small case study, outlining good practice or perhaps just passing on personal wisdom. It also shows how organizations have to develop meaningful ways to learn from their successes and failures. Case studies provide a helpful tool for them to do so. It can be argued that public sector organizations have no lack of studies, enquiries, and *post facto* assessments of performance. These are often very formal or politically charged documents that tend, unfortunately, to focus more on blame than learning. Case studies, which combine the facts of the situation along with the context and lessons learned, provide a more informal, neutral space that encourages learning. Organizations that build this kind of learning into their cultures on a systematic basis are strengthening their resilience capacity through learning.

Organizational Tools for Creating and Distributing Case Studies

People are not used to thinking about what they know. The same can be said for sharing what we know: we seldom sit down and do it in a regular fashion. Organizations are the same. While the business sector has a wide range of cases available, driven by the extensive use of the case study methodology in business schools, there are fewer cases in the public sector. That does not mean that there is a lack of material, just intent. However, there are ways to develop cases applicable to organizational learning in the public sector. It does take leadership and resources of some kind, be it staff time or money. The following is a list of ideas for how organizations can both create and use case studies.

Recognition and Awards

Many public sector organizations seek out recognition for major achievements through awards from professional organizations. In doing so, they document a particularly successful undertaking, sharing the information they gathered in the process. The quality of the knowledge shared varies dramatically across countries and reward systems. For a government manager, however, it pays to see what kinds of efforts are being recognized by colleagues within the public administration profession. It is also possible to convert these submissions into actual cases.

Building the Inventory

At the end of Chapter 2 and in the back matter of this book, a number of public sector case study programs and inventories are listed. It is to the advantage of organizations with a commitment to knowledge management to encourage staff and academics to contribute cases to these inventories.

Using Cases in Staff Training

Central to the adoption of knowledge management is the creation of forums in which to share that knowledge. While current trends are toward web-based concepts, many public organizations have a centralized department or staff members, or a contracted agency, responsible for staff training in the organization as a whole. Case studies are an ideal form for training in this context. Trainers must be grounded in the reality of the government experience as they are providing training directly related to work effectiveness. This is considerably less theoretical than academic education. Also, they are working with employees who are immersed in their jobs, want practical solutions, and fully understand the relationship of learning and context. They want an approach that incorporates the human dimension of the information being taught. Cases provide that mix.

Case Studies 2.0

The reality of knowledge sharing is that it is increasingly digital. The challenge and opportunity for organizations in the twenty-first century is how to use this capacity to share ideas, experience, and information to expand knowledge management. The potential here is enormous. It is well beyond simply posting case studies on an organization's website. That, of course, would be a good first step. Electronic media also enable all those engaged in a department – leaders, managers, employees, and clients – to create cases of their own to share with others. For instance, National Resources Canada, a federal government department rich in technical knowledge, has led the way with the development of an internal 2.0 wiki to foster employee collaboration and knowledge sharing. This includes the sharing of experience through storytelling and informal case studies.[6] Case studies move very quickly into the areas of crowd sourcing, communities of practice, and social networks. Harnessing that in a sufficiently systematic way is a challenge for all public organizations. So, too, is managing the privacy concerns.

Experiential Case Studies in Perspective

Case studies are a great learning tool for all organizations. They permit the transfer of ideas and experience in a way that can meet the needs of individual practitioners. They also permit organizational leadership to capture important stories and learning to make sure that others pick it up. Case studies are not, however, the only way this learning happens. What they bring is an informality and specificity to the knowledge transfer process. Here are some final thoughts to keep in mind when using them:

- A case study focuses on a specific aspect, event, or time horizon in the life of a project or policy. Cases do not cover the whole, but only tell a certain story.
- Each story has one or more learning objectives that can be used for discussion, presentation, or self-reflection.
- The story belongs to someone else, and that should be respected.
- Case writers build cases on respect and trust, not authority.
- Cases are living documents intended for interaction and interpretation. They are not reports of indisputable facts. Indeed, outcomes evolve and

end results may not, upon reflection, appear as positive or negative as at the time of their occurrence.

- Case studies are only as useful as the use to which they are put. Simply writing them is not enough; they transfer nothing without a vehicle, be it class training, electronic sharing, video feeds, or webinars to share the case in live time.

Notes

[1] See, for example, W. D. Eggers and J. O'Leary, *If We Can Put a Man on the Moon . . . Getting Big Things Done in Government* (Boston: Harvard Business Press, 2009). For an interactive application linked to this website, see http://journeyto successmap.com/.

[2] P. S. Vilches Fresneda and S. M. Goulart Gonçalves, Documentation and Information Center Publishing Coordination Brasília, *Formulating a Knowledge Management Policy Federal Public Administration the Brazilian Experience* (Brazil: Chamber of Deputies, 2008).

[3] F. F. Batista, C. O. Quandt, F. F. Pacheco, and J. C. C. Terra, *Gestão do Conhecimento na Administração Pública* [Knowledge Management in Public Administration] (Brasília: Instituto de Pesquisa Econômica Aplicada [IPEA], 2005), Texto para Discussão No. 1095. Available at http://www.ipea.gov.br/pub/td/2005/td_1095.pdf.

[4] For more information, see www.anzsog.edu.au.

[5] M. Collins, "The Role of Case Studies" (Carnegie Mellon University, Pittsburgh, 1999), http://www.ece.cmu.edu/~koopman/des_s99/case_studies/index.html#role.

[6] M. Akerly, "Supporting and Driving Collaboration with Web 2.0," Conference Board of Canada, May 2009.

Part 2

Case Samplers

Case Sampler #1

Reading into History

This case, available with more detail and excellent pictures on the website of NASA's Goddard Space Flight Center at http://www.nasa.gov/centers/goddard/about/organizations/OCKO/casestudies/index.html, shows how well the case method can be adapted to historical circumstances. It also shows how modern tools such as risk analysis can retrospectively be used. This case would work well in any teaching situation, be it academic or organizational.

LAUNCHING THE *VASA*

A lot rode on the men who were building the Swedish gunship *Vasa* in 1626, and those who would sail her. It had been a calamitous decade for the Swedish navy. A dozen of Sweden's largest warships had been captured, wrecked, or scuttled; a violent storm in 1625 had destroyed 10 of those ships, prompting the imperious King Gustav II Adolf to order four new ones. Further losses had dramatically increased the king's impatience with his shipbuilders.

Make It Longer!

The *Vasa* was first ordered as a small, traditional ship, but after numerous change orders from the king it was increased in both size and armament. A 111-foot keel was laid down, but almost immediately work stopped as the king learned that rival Denmark was building a larger ship with two gun decks, a new innovation. The *Vasa*'s keel was ordered to be increased to 135 feet, and the ship was now to include two enclosed gun decks.

No one in Sweden had ever built such a ship, and with the king making constant and ever-louder demands for both larger dimensions and faster delivery, there was no time for plans to be engineered. It was decided that scaling up the 111-foot keel, rather than laying a new, 135-foot keel, would save time.

The shipbuilders added a fourth scarf to lengthen the keel, but the result was narrow in relation to its length and the draft very shallow for a ship of that size. A foot and a half was added to the beam, but because the keel was already laid it had to be added to the uppermost parts of the ship. This raised the center of gravity and contributed to the ship's instability. The shallow keel did not allow sufficient room for the ballast needed to stabilize a ship of that size, and the narrow beam required extra bracing timbers, further reducing room for the ballast.

More Guns!

With a bigger ship, King Gustav demanded more – and bigger – guns, insisting on 64 24-pounders, half on each deck, plus numerous smaller ones. Though it was built for 12-pounders, the upper deck now had to carry the added weight of 24-pounders, which further raised the center of gravity. In the end, the rushed schedule allowed for 48 24-pounders.

Adding to the top-heavy condition: hundreds of ornate, gilded, and painted carvings made of heavy oak, also ordered by the king.

To outshine the Danish ship, no cost was spared, and the *Vasa* became the most expensive ship of its time.

Management Change

In 1626, the head shipbuilder became very ill. While bedridden, he had to share his duties with two others, which led to confusion over project management. Division of responsibility and communication was weak, exacerbated by the king's impatience and ever-changing demands and resulting in further delays. With the largest workforce in Sweden's history essentially running amok, the shipbuilder died in 1627.

At the time, there were no standardized calculations for center of gravity, heeling characteristics, and stability factors. Ship captains learned their ships' characteristics by trial-and-error. Even naval experts believed that the higher and more impressive a ship, and the more guns it carried, the more indestructible the ship would be.

Launch Readiness Test

Finally, all that remained was a test of the *Vasa*'s seaworthiness. In what was called a "lurch" test, the ship's captain and the king's admiral had a skeleton crew of 30 men run from gunwale to gunwale amidships on a windless day in calm harbor waters. After three such sprints, the test was stopped because the ship was rocking so violently that the captain feared it would capsize. The shipbuilders were not present nor were they informed of the test results. No action was taken after the alarming results because the only known corrective course was 'more ballast,' which was not a viable option. Already loaded with 120 tons of ballast, there was no room for more. Even if there had been more room, the additional weight would have put the lower deck gun portals near or below the waterline. As it stood, those ports were only 3 feet above the waterline.

The Launch

It is July 25, 1628. You are the king's admiral. You are under orders to launch today or suffer severe personal and professional consequences. You are being held responsible for the careers of the shipbuilder and shipwright, and the lives of the ship's captain and his 150-man crew. You are also responsible for the image of an expansionist Sweden and its main weapon, the Swedish Navy, now severely crippled by losses during wartime.

Reluctant, but obedient, and unwilling to stall any longer, on August 10, 1628, you order the ship to be pulled away from the wharf. A few sails are raised just as a light breeze picks up to fill the sails. The breeze fills the ship's sails and lifts spirits. The *Vasa* sails about 1,000 yards, heels over, and sinks in view of the entire spectator crowd. Fifty souls are lost along with the entire ship. What went wrong? What would you do differently next time? Fortunately, you have access to some of the risk analyses (appended) done during the project to look for clues and lessons learned. King Gustav was in Poland and out of communication, though he had ordered that the ship be launched by July 25 and "if not, those responsible would be subject to His Majesty's disgrace." Neither the shipwright nor the shipbuilder had been present for the lurch test, and no one had suggested any ideas for increasing the *Vasa*'s stability. You know that upon the king's return there will be a royal board of inquiry, and you will have some tough questions to answer. You start thinking about them now to prepare yourself for what lies ahead. You decide to call together a small group of your trusted advisors and together you mull over these questions:

Who is responsible for this catastrophe?

- Were there any inappropriate risks that should not have been taken? How can these be identified and mitigated in future shipbuilding initiatives?
- How can unknown areas be addressed beyond relying on the shipbuilder's personal expertise? How do we advance into areas that are unknown?
- How could the communications between the king, the shipbuilders, and the navy command be improved for the contracting, building, and

delivery of future warships in a timely, on-schedule, and within-budget manner?

- What is the most important thing we can do to prevent this type of disaster from happening again?

Sample Risk Profiles

<table>
<tr><td colspan="4">Risk Title: Synchronization of Core Ship and the Gun Deck Architectures</td><td>Owner: Shipbuilder</td></tr>
<tr><td colspan="5">Risk Statement: Given the existing challenges the Vasa project is addressing and the instability in the Vasa configuration, there is a possibility that the gun deck (war-fighting capability) project will not be able to maintain synchronized design analysis cycles leading up to an agreed architecture.</td></tr>
<tr><td>Likelihood: 3</td><td>Safety: 0</td><td>Performance: 3</td><td>Schedule: 5</td><td>Cost: 4</td></tr>
<tr><td colspan="5">Context: Both the ship core architecture (keel, beam, tonnage, and ballast) and the gun deck (armaments, configuration, gun mix, and mass) have been redesigned and continue to undergo revisions and requirements changes. This instability of requirements makes it difficult to synchronize the architectures and will likely require rework, and/or compromises that could affect the success of the mission. For example: The armaments command is requiring all 24-pounders (both gun decks) to standardize on gun fixtures and ammunition for efficient use in battle.</td></tr>
<tr><td colspan="5">Status: Upper gun deck ports already installed are too small for 24-pounders (Fall 1627). Schedule interchange meeting to compromise on upper deck guns.</td></tr>
<tr><td colspan="3">Mitigation Plan: Attempt to synchronize the design and load cycles of both ship and weapons.</td><td colspan="2">Fallback Plan: Install more carvings of Norse Gods on the ship.</td></tr>
</table>

<table>
<tr><td colspan="4">Risk Title: Vasa Vehicle Test Environment Limitations</td><td>Owner: Shipbuilder</td></tr>
<tr><td colspan="5">Risk Statement: Given that the current Vasa design concept (modified) has high stability-test levels (load testing) and the adaptation of existing or modified structures (timbers) and components (guns, decorative art) is intended for use in many Vasa applications, there is a possibility that the Vasa project may incur schedule slips and increased cost due to subsystem failures requiring more system-level test cycles to achieve qualification.</td></tr>
<tr><td>Likelihood: 4</td><td>Safety: 1</td><td>Performance: 3</td><td>Schedule: 5</td><td>Cost: 3</td></tr>
<tr><td colspan="5">Context: Historically some ship designs have failed (sunk due to instability) and required some redesign. Critical stability tests are driven by core ship-design issues. Current schedule analysis indicates significant overlap between subsystem qualifications and completion of seaworthiness build, assembly, and test cycles.</td></tr>
<tr><td colspan="5">Status: Vasa project is made the highest priority by order of the king (November 1625). Admiral Fleming to conduct a prelaunch lurch test with 30 sailors (July 1627).</td></tr>
<tr><td colspan="3">Mitigation Plan: Results of lurch test to be analyzed for adjusting ballast before launch.</td><td colspan="2">Fallback Plan: Install more carvings of Norse Gods on the ship.</td></tr>
</table>

<table>
<tr><td colspan="4">Risk Title: Complexity of Interprogram Management Structure</td><td>Owner: Shipbuilder</td></tr>
<tr><td colspan="5">Risk Statement: Given the complexity of the interprogram management structure in the Swedish navy and the historic cultural differences between civilian, naval, and royal offices, there is a possibility that integration of the Vasa project will be negatively impacted.</td></tr>
<tr><td>Likelihood: 2</td><td>Safety: 1</td><td>Performance: 2</td><td>Schedule: 2</td><td>Cost: 2</td></tr>
<tr><td colspan="5">Context: There is the built-in complexity of the Vasa organization and the work packages-making system-interfaces complex. This is most apparent between the shipbuilding team and the king's court. Requirements, design, and implementation processes, procedures, and formal office-to-office agreements have not been documented. There are multiple approaches from different quarters in solving a common technical risk. The resulting impact to the Vasa project is in not meeting the schedule and inefficient implementation due to cultural differences and drivers with foci that are different from that of the mission.</td></tr>
<tr><td colspan="5">Status: Awaiting word from the king on design changes (July 1626). Death of Master Shipwright Hybertsson increases risk (Spring 1627)?</td></tr>
<tr><td colspan="3">Mitigation Plan: The Vasa project will watch this risk to see if it becomes an issue.</td><td colspan="2">Fallback Plan: Install more carvings of Norse Gods on the ship.</td></tr>
</table>

<table>
<tr><td colspan="4">Risk Title: Timely Availability of Skills/Skills Mix and Cultural Changes</td><td>Owner: Shipbuilder</td></tr>
<tr><td colspan="5">Risk Statement: Given the current skill availability, mix, and culture, there is a possibility that we may not be able to execute a new shipbuilding project in a timely manner.</td></tr>
<tr><td>Likelihood: 4</td><td>Safety: 0</td><td>Performance: 0</td><td>Schedule: 4</td><td>Cost: 0</td></tr>
<tr><td colspan="5">Context: The combination of the two different-sized ships being built simultaneously, the ongoing war (affordability questions), the mix of older shipbuilders and new warfare strategies is pushing the project outside of known experience bases in size, weight, and operations' designs.</td></tr>
<tr><td colspan="5">Status: Interviewing key stakeholders for better understanding (July 1626). Schedule slips are unavoidable due to changing requirements (Spring 1627).</td></tr>
<tr><td colspan="3">Mitigation Plan: Research; interview the key stakeholders to identify skills gaps and cultural differences.</td><td colspan="2">Fallback Plan: Install more carvings of Norse Gods on the ship.</td></tr>
</table>

Case Sampler #2

Case Study Sample: Straightforward or Lively?

Examine the following two examples of the same case, one set out in a factual manner and the other in a more anecdotal format. Which case is more effective in telling the story and presenting the dilemma?

Version A

A teacher was instructing a large class of students in introductory modern political theory at a large urban university. She was using a version of cooperative learning where students worked in small groups throughout the term. She gave daily quizzes, first individually and then in groups. The professor had a habit of leaving the classroom during the quizzes. All went well until the last day of class when she heard from one of her best students that cheating had occurred during the quizzes. When she gave out peer evaluation forms for the students to rank their teammates, she gained additional information. Two students who knew each other in adjoining groups had been cheating. Six separate students wrote about how the two friends had cheated and that they had been told to stop by their teammates but to no avail. There were no more class periods left, only the final exam. What should the teacher do?

Version B

"I couldn't stand it! I had to move. They were cheating. I study hard to get my A, and they were cheating. What are you going to do about it?"

Political science professor Margaret Blake looked hard at the young woman standing in front of her desk. Paula was one of her best students. Margaret

---

This case was written by Andrew Graham for use in the School of Policy Studies at Queen's University.

had asked her why she had suddenly moved from one table to another during the daily quiz.

"Lang, the guy in the group next to us, writes his multiple choice answers in large letters on his quiz paper. He holds it up for Jack who is in our group to see while you are out of the room. We all told them to stop, but they keep doing it."

Margaret replied, "I wish you had told me sooner, we could have done something. Today is the last day of class. Friday we have the final exam. There isn't much we can do now. Well, at least today we are having the peer evaluation where you rank the contributions of the rest of the members of your group. Be sure you write down your complaint."

"I guarantee that a lot of us will complain."

Paula's words came true. Six students wrote pointedly about the cheating between the two Asian students. One student in Jack's group was especially angry: "Jack is never prepared. He comes to lab whenever he feels like it, and he and his buddy cheat every single day. Did you see how badly Jack did on the quiz when you stood behind him? And he always changes his answers on his bubble sheet and pretends they were scored wrong. I HATE CHEATERS! AARRGH! You better not bring the group's participation mark down just because of one jerk."

Margaret sat in her office, stunned. She always thought that group learning prevented this sort of thing; otherwise, she never would have left the room during the quizzes. Now what? Paula's last words rang in her ears, "They were cheating. What are you going to do about it?"

Case Sampler #3

Ethical Challenges: Simple but Complex

Cases do not have to be long to be both demanding and, at times, deceptively complex. The following short case contains seeds of a public service ethical and managerial dilemma, although stated in a fairly story-like way.

What are the variables at play here? Is there a right and wrong? What are the risks of action, of inaction? What would you do?

THE MINISTERIAL DIRECTIVE, OR WAS THAT A SUGGESTION?

The newly elected government, after two terms in opposition, was going about the process of settling into office. The first order of business for the new Minister was to meet his senior advisors from the Ministry and get briefed on the issues of the day. His Permanent Secretary led the briefings, which went on for several hours. The Minister felt he was being treated well and in a professional manner. At the end of the sessions, he asked to see the Permanent Secretary privately.

"I wanted to thank you for the top-notch briefings I received today. I can see that your people have read our party's platform carefully. I am glad they have started to get their heads around where we want to go."

"We take these first encounters very seriously, Minister. We want to respond to the government's direction and ensure that it can be well implemented. Of course, that will mean my advising you against certain courses of action. I can assure you that will only be after a thorough look at the facts and some effort to try to find a way to meet your objectives."

This case was written by Andrew Graham for use in the School of Policy Studies at Queen's University.

"Oh, I am sure we will have a few of those "Yes Minister" conversations – or do you call them telling truth to power? Well, all is proceeding in good form. There is, however, one matter of real concern to me. It is probably the only area where I am very uncomfortable. Your Assistant Permanent Secretary for Policy, Alice Dodds, gave me nothing but misery when I was in opposition. She led the way before the House committee during expenditure review. She was the author of that policy initiative on cross-subsidization that I opposed so strongly and that we intend to turn around. Mr. Secretary, I do not believe that I can work with her. I do not want her on my team of senior bureaucratic advisors. I am expecting you to take the necessary actions to make it so. I know I have no authority on this matter. That is for the Civil Service Commission and not Cabinet. You figure it out. I really see no other way but to act, and to act now."

Case Sampler #4

Cases That Create Group Discussion and Analytical Challenges

The following case is one that requires that groups work together to build criteria for selecting certain budget options and then apply their criteria to a number of expenditure options during the budgetary process for a policy department. It engages groups in the real-life process of setting budget priorities.

COMPETING BUSINESS CASES: THE BUDGET OF THE METRO POLICE SERVICE

Background

You are a member of the Police Service Board that oversees the Metro Police Service. One of your responsibilities is to approve the budget for the Service before it is forwarded to the municipality to be incorporated into the overall budget. As such, you must weigh the needs of the Service with the need for fiscal restraint. The municipality cannot overturn your approval unless it chooses to go to the province. As you are charged by law with the effective management of the Police Service, you will have to balance a number of factors in coming to your conclusions.

The Chief has presented you with a series of business cases for improving service. These are over and above the normal increases in costs due to salary negotiations and factors such as increased cost of fuel. These business cases represent changes to service levels as well as the capacity of the service in technical areas. This is a normal part of the budget process. The Chief has put forward these ideas as an opening round of informal discussions about priorities. These have come out of the Chief's internal strategic planning sessions. While he will come back to the Board in the next round with his own prioritized list, he has developed this process to sound out the Board.

This case was written by Andrew Graham for use in the School of Policy Studies at Queen's University.

He also has found that, as the Board has been supportive but challenging, he has developed a good rapport and trust with the members. Therefore, he is comfortable sounding them out. In their turn, they have learned the value of good questioning before making a decision and not taking everything the Chief says as final.

One of the Board's concerns is that the Police Service wants too many new projects funded. It has had to deal with both political and public criticisms of increases driven by staff salaries, which have outpaced those of other municipal employees. While it accepts this as part of its lot, it feels that this reduces its capacity to support too many initiatives. There was a great sucking of air when the list of new ideas floated below was put in front of the Board. The Chair noted that after these discussions, the Chief would have to consider some form of prioritization to reduce the list to make it more saleable.

Your Assignment

This is a two-stage exercise and needs to be recorded and reported in that fashion. The criteria that you create should be applied to each business case as presented. The application of those criteria should be explicit and clear when you make your presentations.

Each team will appoint a recorder and a rapporteur.

Assignment 1: Developing Criteria for Assessment

As a team, you will develop a series of questions and issues that you would raise in assessing each of these business cases. Your criteria should relate to good budgeting practice as a whole. What are the kinds of things that would concern you when looking at this "shopping list," as one Board member dubbed it? Take into account (a) all the factors addressed in the discussion on budgets, (b) issues that you would want addressed as part of responsible oversight of a large public sector budget, and (c) broader issues of public sector policy that may arise in reviewing this list.

As a team, you will develop a checklist for comparing the various business cases. What factors would you want to see in place to be able to effectively compare and prioritize these cases? You are not restricted to the information provided. While your checklist should be applied to all the cases, you may with these examples ask specific questions that will provide you with a better basis for comparison.

Assignment 2: More Work Needed

From a budget perspective, the Board does not feel that many of the key financial let alone operational and strategic questions have been properly addressed in these short submissions. Formulate a list of questions that you would send back to the Chief to enable you to better understand the nature of each request.

Information on these business cases is very high level. Your job is to prepare a short presentation on questions that you would ask from a budgeting perspective. Take into account the following (not exhaustive list – add your own):

- What information is missing?
- What assumptions about strategy and direction of the Police Service are being made? Are they correct?
- What information is available about direct and indirect costs in the short and long term?
- What are the risks being addressed in this proposal?
- What performance measures – both quantitative and qualitative – are present or lacking?
- How would you set up criteria for sorting these various business cases, even if they all proved to be good in themselves?

The Shopping List

The Chief has presented the following business cases, saying that he supports them all in principle, but recognizes that there are budget constraints. He has not prioritized the list. It is also clear that, after this review by the Board, he will be resubmitting the proposals in a more formal way.

1. Creating a Motorcycle Unit for Gang Crime Unit

It is proposed that 15 new officers along with the necessary machinery be funded to increase street surveillance of gang activity in high-crime areas. In addition to gang activity in the downtown core, where traffic at night remains a problem, there has been significant growth in gang activity in the newer suburbs, especially in neighbourhoods with high concentrations of single ethnic groups. The Chief believes that greater mobility will increase the overall police presence in those neighbourhoods, and will also enable more speedy interventions at gang events. "Right now, we need presence as much as anything," the Chief stated. "Motorcycles provide the most effective means of doing this. Neighbourhoods around certain schools would greatly benefit from more frequent mobile patrols. This is the way to do it." Presently, the municipality of OZ has a small motorcycle unit for traffic purposes. However, it is underresourced in this area compared with other municipalities of the same size. Council and a number of neighbourhood groups have pressured both the Board and the Chief on gang activity.

2. Purchasing a New Helicopter

It is proposed that the Service acquire a new helicopter due to the aging of the existing one and the effectiveness of helicopter presence during demonstrations as well as for traffic control. However, the Chief is also linking this to the need for better emergency response, especially with respect to terrorism, which is an expansion of the use for the helicopter. In his request to the Board, he estimated the new chopper and all the necessary components would cost about $2.4 million, but the sale of an older model helicopter in the private market would net about $400,000. He said the old model was quickly approaching the point at which it would need an extensive overhaul that would cost more than it is currently worth. Furthermore, the new AS 350 B2 Eurocopter would be able to carry three more passengers, and accommodate more equipment such as infrared sensors and extra radios. "The copter program has been a great success. It has increased our response capacity tremendously. This is just a capital replacement item, in effect," said the Chief. However, it is a hefty one that will certainly attract a lot of attention if it is put forward. This is the first time that the Board has been made aware of the need to replace the helicopter, even though it is a major capital item. The present capital and equipment plan has not addressed this item.

3. Expand 911 Facilities and Staff

The population is increasingly using 911 calls for many forms of emergency and non-emergency questions and problems. Citizen-assist calls now constitute almost 40 percent of all first calls. This volume has not decreased even though the City has introduced a 311 general information call centre on an experimental basis. The current staff and facilities are stressed. Expansion would be costly if it is to meet demand. However, the current public concern with failure to respond adequately has hit this Service and City. A few new positions have been approved in the current fiscal year, but this is not seen as adequate. As the Chief stated in his presentation to the Board,

> While a proposal to belatedly add a few positions was a nice gesture, it doesn't go far enough. That's exactly what happened after the release of a study two years ago that actually recommended adding eighteen positions. There are recognized standards for assessing staffing needs for 911 centres. Let's put them to work now, not later. If we are indeed short of dispatchers by those standards, it's time to get moving. It will take months to make the hires and train new dispatchers, and we're wasting time having committee meetings and pondering burning even more taxpayer dollars for new studies while calls go waiting. One thing is clear after weeks of public concern and expressed by almost 100 people at a public hearing Monday night – 911 is a priority.

The Chief also identified the capital needed to upgrade the workstations. New equipment being used in the United States, with each station costing about $75,000, provides much faster information on more screens with automatic linkage to GPS. The current lodging of the 911 facilities within the police budget is based on historic practice. However, the majority of cities of comparable profile have created autonomous 911 units to serve fire, police, and emergency services calls.

4. Creating a Crime Prevention Unit Focused on Immigrant Populations

The Service wants to expand its outreach to immigrant communities that have little contact with police. It sees real gaps in immigrant services and proposes a unit of ten uniformed officers and fifteen non-uniformed specialists in race relations to improve community contact. "Successful integration is the best crime prevention method," said the Chief, adding that the police must increase their intercultural competency to better function in a diverse society. This new unit would have a number of roles, including in-house training, outreach, and patrol. The Chief was unable to provide information on the crime rates within these communities. "One of our problems is that we have little or no access into these groups. They distrust police, based on their experiences in their home countries." No information was available on how various ethnic groups would respond. A local academic recently made a speech calling targeted ethnic policing "racism dressed up as caring."

5. Expanding the Police Service Training Centre

The present facility is used for induction training and follow-up mandated officer training. It is old and inadequate. The gym and the firing range are well below current practice and standards. The indoor firing range has drawn some complaints from nearby residents. The Chief proposes building a state-of-the-art touchstone building with ample space both for training and for the many meetings and conferences now put on by the Service. The City could use the facility on a payback basis. The new training centre would include classrooms, a gymnasium, a firearms simulator, a driving simulator, and a pool for water safety training. The current facilities appear to meet basic needs for class space, although the rooms are not well lit and the equipment is pre-PowerPoint quality. The City has a stock of buildings, some of which might be repurposed, although the Chief and his head of training are opposing this. It is uncertain what the capital costs of repurposing would be. Further, there are two community colleges within the Police Service jurisdiction, both with large campuses. One has a police science program that provides a number of recruits on a regular basis.

Reminder of Your Job: Do Not Jump to Conclusions or Decisions

Remember, your job is to initiate the budgetary thinking by asking questions that reflect your understanding of what a budget is, how priorities are set, and what needs to be taken into account in weighing these alternatives.

Your second job is to assess, based on the information provided, whether these issues could be delayed for future budgets. Also, what additional work might need to be done to strengthen the rationale for each proposal?

Case Sampler #5

Cases with Complex Narratives

The following case is an example of a complex, narrative-type case that involves many elements at one time. Consider how the narrative adds contextual information. Consider as well the number of different perspectives that are added.

PROBLEM EMPLOYEE OR PROBLEM BOSS? CHANGE, RESISTANCE, PERFORMANCE, AND LEADERSHIP

The New Guy

Paolo Rodriquez has just been appointed Director of the Environmental Policy Unit (EPU) in the policy branch of the Department of Natural Resources (DNR) for the Province of Contentment. This is his first big move into management. He has supervised people before and brings to the EPU a reputation for being high-energy, positive and a team player, at least among his peers.

Paolo also sees this job as a way to break into the policy world. He has spent a lot of time working for other executives as an assistant. He has worked in a deputy minister's office and is known to be politically sensitive.

Paolo is young for this promotion – 32. He has moved quickly. He is relatively unknown to his staff as most of his experience in DNR was in other branches. He has also worked in other departments.

The EPU is a relatively small unit of 24 employees. Reporting to Paolo are three supervisors, two of them responsible for policy areas and the other for the small administrative support unit. All administrative support is centralized for the unit. The EPU gets all of its finance and human resources support from the branch specialists who report to the assistant deputy minister (ADM).

Both of the policy area supervisors, Deidre and Ken, had applied for the director's job. Both have longer work experience than Paolo, but with

---

This case study by Andrew Graham is also part of the IPAC inventory.

considerably less diversity. They have tended to stay put, specializing in environmental issues.

Man with a Mission

The ADM, Policy – Georgina – has been pretty dissatisfied with the EPU for some time. She has tried to get this sensitive area for the province more attuned with greater public sensitivity to the environment. She has also tried to bring environmental issues, especially community engagement and integrated planning, onto the broader natural resources agenda. She has not felt well supported by the existing team. She sees Paolo as someone who "gets it" and who she can guide to become one of her leading managers.

In offering Paolo the job, Georgina made it clear that she expects changes. She felt that the issue was not necessarily one of the people, but of the culture of the unit. She therefore made it clear that she wanted changes, but she did not want a bloodbath – to use her words. "Wake these people up. Bring in the big picture. Make them more attuned to selling their messages, which I see buried in long, useless briefing material, to the rest of the branch and the department."

In accepting the job, Paolo saw this as a big opportunity to show himself and his potential. He certainly understood the big picture. He knew that he would have a big job convincing the EPU that there had to be changes. He was unsure about what to do first and how. He also knew that he was walking into some pretty murky waters.

But Paolo believed in the power of energy and in personal leadership. He felt that the good staff would be happy to have a stronger hand.

The Ken and Deidre Show

Upon his arrival, Paolo did a walk around of his little share of the cubicles on the third floor of the DNR building. He then asked to see his three supervisors in his office for a brief chat.

Before he could get going, both Ken and Deidre launched into a fairly bitter attack on how little respect the advice that they produces was given by the ADM, let alone the department as a whole. "Nobody with in-depth technical ability gets an ear around here, especially on environmental issues. We are always seen as complicating people's lives. They just want to run parks."

Paolo saw this as an opening and leapt into it – all the way. "That is exactly why I am here, I guess. I am pretty sure the ADM wants to turn this around too."

Ken and Deidre looked at each other and then at Paolo for clarification. "I have to take some time to sort this out for myself, but I certainly have direction to improve our performance here. I also have direction to make our voice more respected."

Reactions to this statement seemed to split Ken and Deidre and therein the tale moves on. Deidre said, "Well, it's about time! When do we start?" Ken said, "Not so fast. What do you mean and where do we fit in?"

Paolo replied, "With me, I hope."

The Paolo Project

For the next few months, Paolo seemed to be hitting all the right buttons. He started a team-building process inside the EPU – a day away, a planning session, and some team-building work. He caught very clearly the message that most of the workers had seen themselves as apart from DNR and not respected.

Without any new resources available to him, he could not hire new staff, and so he was limited in how much more he could ask people to do.

However, he started to try to move them out of their safety zone and into the broader department. He got staff named to a variety of committees across the department. He started to work on some strategic pieces for the ADM to present to the Senior Management Committee. He worked with other directors more closely.

Paolo was high energy and expected all of his staff to be as well. Very soon they began to complain that all of these committees and strategic planning sessions were getting in the way of their real work. They continued to produce very thoughtful and detailed documents criticizing departmental policy for its lack of an environmental vision. Briefing notes of 15 to 20 pages continued to be the norm, although Paolo kept asking them to be edited down.

Paolo also clarified the duties of Ken and Deidre. Because of her enthusiasm, Paolo asked Deidre to manage the relationships within the department. She would carry the horizontal work. Ken would focus on policy analysis – his specialty.

Paolo made it clear to Ken that effective communications were as important as substantive analysis. Ken commented to his staff, "I suppose he wants to boil these complex ideas into a 10-page PowerPoint presentation!"

Things Stop Going So Well

The situation in the unit started to show signs of strain. Some staff started looking for other jobs. Sick leave was on the rise. Fewer staff were available to work long hours in urgent situations.

Then one day Deidre stormed into Paolo's office and said, "I just can't do this anymore. I set this stuff up, I send my folks and we get laughed at. Our material stinks. The messages are there but lost in poor presentation. That's when we have something to present. Our reports are so detailed that often we don't get them done in time for the meeting. We're becoming a joke around here."

Deidre made it clear that she liked working with Paolo but was fed up with her present role. She was thinking of moving on. There were plenty of positions for a person of her skills. Besides, her recent high profile in the department had already led to a few offers from other directors.

Deidre said nothing directly, but she hinted that Ken was the problem. She felt that she had risen to the challenge that Paolo had put forward, but that Ken had not.

Paolo had not missed this either. Ken was still taking too long to get the work done. He had not joined in the broader role, but retreated into the analytical role, consulting even less than before. His work habits had not changed. Rather, the long memos continued, and so did the overly complicated arguments that distorted the message and turned people off.

Paolo found himself increasingly editing material. Every re-edit session had become a showdown with Ken. If Ken was not there, his staff would go to him afterwards. They saw Paolo as an uninformed careerist using them to get his next promotion. They thought he simply did not understand environmental issues. A few friends around DNR were telling Paolo that the two policy supervisors were sending such different signals that they wondered who was right. Deidre seemed to be promising better advice and team playing. Ken seemed to be rehearsing the holier than thou version of environmental neglect without offering much in the way of advice. Further, they were having little impact on policy matters.

Ken's Performance

Paolo had to decide if Ken was up to the job that he had given him. His performance had certainly slipped since Paolo's arrival. It was being noticed. Questions like "What's up with Ken?" and "I thought that at least he knew his stuff, even if he kept it to himself" started being voiced.

Ken himself was not sending many signals of enjoyment at work. He tended to be non-communicative at EPU meetings, seldom suggesting agenda items. He voiced neither opposition nor support for Paolo's directions.

Ken was not ambitious, even though he had applied for the director's position. He was not well connected within the government, having worked in this one area for over ten years. He was, however, proud of his expertise in environmental issues. He hoped someday to teach. He saw himself as an intellectual.

Ken never gave a specific cause for concern about his work. He was on top of the substance of the files, but everything seemed to go into slow motion. Always there was a reason for things not happening, a defence, an explanation. Seldom did Paolo hear about it being solved.

Increasingly, Ken's isolation started to show. His staff were often left to work on policy issues on their own. Deidre would sometime informally discuss issues with them when they needed help. Ken would often vigorously re-edit papers and briefing notes, adding considerable length and detail. He also would make sarcastic, hand-written comments on the drafts that were becoming increasingly hurtful to staff.

Some staff had already talked to the union about these comments, which they regarded as harassment. Ken was also a union member, being only at the supervisory level. So the union contacted Paolo with the suggestion that he sort this out internally. If he failed to do so, he might have a harassment charge on his hands.

Once or twice, the ADM asked, "What's up with Ken? He's always been an OK guy, a bit aloof, but OK. But now he's cutting up his staff, like he's blaming them for something. Has he got a problem with you, Paolo?"

In spite of all this, Ken was civil and professional with Paolo. He never confronted him when Paolo put forward a new idea. He simply did not deliver or, more often, the timing and quality were the issue.

Deidre increasingly withdrew from pushing horizontal and departmental involvement. She had been burned once too often. She liked Ken, and they had been through a fair bit of time together. She felt sorry for him. She could see he was unhappy but could not figure out what to do about it. She like Paolo, too, but was unsure about him. He seemed to want to go in the right direction, but was it for flash or for impact?

What Does Paolo Do?

Walking out of a departmental managers' meeting one day, Paolo overheard a couple of senior advisors laughing. "Well, if we really want to put a stop to this proposal, let's bring in the EPU. They still slow things down better than anyone! Having Paolo there just makes us feel better about it."

Paolo was almost sick. He had failed to change things and was becoming part of the joke.

Paolo knew he had let things drag on too long. Ken was the problem. He had to confront him, but how? If he went at Ken directly, he would start a war of words. Regardless of the side comments and the ADM's observations, Ken had always received high ratings in his performance appraisals – when he got them. Timeliness was never part of his objectives for improvement. Good communication was not, either. In fact, Ken had written his objectives for his former supervisors. Paulo had just not had time to get on top of that item.

Paolo was smart enough to know that long service does count for something. Ken was a problem, but not that much of a problem.

Paolo also knew that he had to address the sarcastic remarks that had so upset staff. If he failed to do so, he would be as responsible as Ken for the harassment charge.

Paolo was new at this. In fact, he was a relatively inexperienced manager who had never dealt with a problem employee. He also was reluctant to talk to his boss about this, at least until he had a plan. She was tough and would not tolerate poor managers for long.

Paolo turned to the human resources advisor for the branch. "Ken acts like I am some sort of Philistine, spoiling his pure policy work," Paolo said. "He seems to react through passive resistance." The HR advisor, Gloria, asked: "Does he really know what you expect of him?" Paolo felt that his direction had been good. He wasn't ready to let Ken off the hook on that front. But Gloria pressed on: "You went in there to make some of the changes that Georgina wanted. If Ken can't measure up, then something has to happen. But the burden of proof seems to be with you right now. His performance appraisals are good. By the way, one is overdue. His general work record is good. However, that harassment thing can't be left to fester. You need to think through a strategy before you do anything."

Paolo felt as if the ball had been firmly tossed back into his court. He knew she was right. HR people only advise: they cannot do the manager's job. But what was that job right now?

Case Study Challenge

The problem employee is a major challenge to managers. However, where they most often fail in dealing with problem performance is their failure to use the skills that got them into management in the first place: an ability to analyze and quickly judge what the situation is, an ability to understand the views of others, an ability to set directions, an ability to set goals, monitor performance and provide feedback.

1. Applying these abilities, analyze the situation at hand. Provide a diagnostic of this situation: What is going on here?
2. Suggest a course of action for Paolo to follow with respect to his own management style, his relationship with Ken, and his relationship with other staff of his unit.

Case Sampler #6

Sample Open-Ended Teaching Case

This case from the IPAC Case Study Series offers the teacher the opportunity to pursue a number of potential areas of discussion. The case presents a specific problem, but with a number of alternative approaches. The emphasis in this case is not on the solutions but the value and strategies behind them.

VALUES AND HARD DECISIONS

by Lynne Siemens and Reg Toews

Abstract

A regional health authority (RHA) is facing a budget deficit of $3 million in its upcoming fiscal year. The CEO and board face a series of decisions as they discuss the possible approval of a deficit budget. The board must first determine the values that it holds important and then use those values to determine whether to run a deficit budget (when the government has stated that it will not pick up a deficit), close hospitals, and change services and/or fees to the public. The decisions encompass both large and small policy issues. It is a budgeting case without numbers.

Background

You, as a member of the board of a rural health authority (RHA), are reviewing a draft budget for the upcoming fiscal year. The numbers as they presently stand project a deficit of $3 million, part of which is a $1 million carry-over from the present fiscal year. You realize that before the board can begin to determine if and where cuts might be made, you have to understand the board's collective values: what is important to you and your region in terms of health care. Only then can you make the necessary decisions regarding the future.

History

Ten years ago, the provincial government divided responsibility for health care within the province between the government and ten newly created health authorities, each responsible for a region of the province. The government remains responsible for funding, planning, and implementing the strategic direction for health care in the province. Through the Department of Health, it also sets the essential services that must be provided by each health region. It plays a role evaluating and funding these services.

The regions are responsible for the creation, integration and delivery of health services within their region based on their particular needs. The types of programs delivered by a typical health authority include:

- hospitals;
- personal care homes;
- public health;
- emergency medical services;
- home care;
- mental health;
- midwifery;
- palliative care; and
- services to seniors.

The RHA was formed when the first board was established with members drawn from the local community. The members were and continue to be lawyers, teachers, retired individuals, and business people. The CEO and four-member management team were hired soon thereafter.

Vision and Values

One of the first actions of the 13-member board was to set the vision, values, and objectives for the region. This occurred at an all-day retreat. With the help of a facilitator, the members discussed the values that they felt were most important to health and health care. They discussed many of the complaints they had about the current health delivery system in the region and possible ways to improve it. They also focused on the positive aspects of the system and ways to build on these. At the end of the retreat, the board members agreed on the following vision, values, and objectives:

- *Vision*: optimizing the health of the region through partnerships
- *Values*: integrity, accessibility, responsiveness, respect, and accountability
- *Objectives*:
  - To improve general health;
  - To provide efficient and effective health care;

- To promote reasonable expectations among the public regarding health care delivery;
- To develop tools to assess and monitor care quality, health service usage, and cost effectiveness; and
- To promote the development and delivery of alternative and less expensive services.

The vision, values, and objectives are confirmed yearly at a board retreat, where new board members also learn about the RHA's history and are initiated into its vision and values.

These vision, values, and objectives are also reinforced in the five-year strategic plan. The key health strategies relate to:

- Ensuring that quality basic services are delivered in the region at an optimum level;
- Providing programs and services to vulnerable population groups and service priorities in mental health and accessibility;
- Providing services within the region; and
- Focusing on overall health, not on health care.

The board has used its values and objectives to guide past decisions. Some examples include:

- Increased investment in personal care homes to keep seniors in the community;
- Rejection of the closing of a small hospital in order to keep services accessible; and
- Increased investment in public health projects to improve overall health of the population.

Services

When the RHA was formed, the board assumed responsibility for:

- 4 hospitals (owned and operated);
- 3 personal care homes (owned and operated);
- 4 personal care homes (operated under contract);
- 11 ambulances based at 5 stations; and
- Programs in public health, home care, mental health, midwifery, and telehealth.

At the time of establishment, the region had the lowest number of hospital beds per capita of all regions within the province. After a review of the current and future needs of the region, the board determined there were no excess beds.

Challenges

The region, covering 9,000 square kilometres, has been undergoing rapid population growth of approximately 5 percent annually for the past five years. The current population is 55,000 and projected to increase to 85,000 by 2025. The population is divided among 15 municipalities.

The main areas of population growth have been the young and old. Children under the age of 15 comprise 25 percent of the population. Part of this growth is the result of a recent immigration wave from Europe and Central and South America. These immigrants have a tendency toward large families, meaning that the region has the highest birth rate in the province. This puts pressure on a variety of services and programs in the region, ranging from obstetrics and prenatal and postpartum care, to immunization and school-based programs. The level of services will have to increase by 25 percent in five years to meet the projected growth.

The other portion of the population that is growing is individuals over 65 years of age. At this point, this group is 11 percent of the population and it is expected that the number of seniors will increase by 50 percent by 2009 and double by 2025. This group is increasingly dependent on public health services, personal care homes, home care programs, and ambulances. The board is facing several big challenges regarding this age group. The first relates to the number of beds available relative to the population. There is a deficit of 25 beds in personal care homes, and the deficit will increase to 65 beds in 2010. Another issue is that the personal care homes are in serious need of capital improvements to meet the health needs of this group. Finally, staff levels at the personal care homes (and hospitals) are at minimal levels and in danger of falling below the provincial Health Department guidelines.

Budget Details

The RHA operates with a $45 million budget: it receives 90 percent from the provincial government. Another 8 percent comes from non-insured income and 2 percent from ambulance fees. The level of provincial funding will increase by 12 percent in the new fiscal year, though costs are anticipated to grow by 15 percent.

The region has been traditionally underfunded on a per capita basis when compared to other health authorities within the province. It has the second lowest per capita base funding in the province. The funding gap is particularly large when compared with funding levels for the urban health authority. The region has also found that the province is willing to support capital projects, but not operating costs.

The provincial Department of Health has stated to all health authorities that it will not cover any deficits. Its position is that all authorities receive adequate levels of funding and are able to balance their budgets.

The board asked the CEO to develop a draft budget to facilitate discussion. The first draft of the budget predicted a $2 million deficit, increasing to $3 million when the short fall of the previous fiscal year is included. The management team made typical cuts to costs, which included a 5 percent reduction in travel costs, a 2 percent reduction in office supplies and a 5 percent reduction in food costs. This led to a savings of $300,000. It has become clear that the only way to produce a balanced budget is to drastically alter services levels. This could include closure of one or more hospitals or care homes.

There are some options for increasing revenue and/or reducing costs. The region operates one of the two travel health clinics in the province for people who travel outside the country. The clinic has traditionally operated to meet the travel needs of the region. As mentioned above, there are a large number of immigrants who travel to visit family abroad. In addition, many residents travel abroad for humanitarian reasons. To date, the fees charged do not cover costs. The board can decide to either cut the service or increase the fees to match the user fees charged by the other travel health clinic in the province.

The other option for increased revenues focuses on ambulance costs related to interfacility transfers. An inter-facility transfer is one where the patient is returned to the originating site within 24 hours. Presently, the RHA pays for these transfers, but has found that the number of transfers have been increasing over time, partly because transfers originating from the emergency room to another location have been included. This inclusion is not policy. The costs are $100,000, which could be transferred to the patient.

Public Demands

At monthly public meetings, the region's residents have been very vocal in their demand for local services. Despite the region's proximity to the province's largest city and its range of health services, people are consulting local doctors, using the region's hospitals, and demanding services for seniors, among other things. In recent surveys, the residents highlighted their priorities as prevention, mental health, and availability/accessibility of core services. The board has been watching these trends and evaluating ways to meet them.

Political Context

The government's focus is on reducing taxes, balancing the budget, and reducing the debt. A key part of this is keeping a lid on increasing health care costs while developing a system that is based on outcomes and wellness. At the same time, the government realizes that people want local services that clearly meet their needs. The government's position with regard to the health authorities is that the authorities are adequately funded and the government will not cover deficits.

Action Required

The next board meeting is next week and the major item of discussion will be the budget. You will be receiving the revised budget tomorrow, but before it comes, you want to review your approach to budget cuts.

You will need to give thought to the following issues:

- The RHA's vision and values;
- Feasibility of running a deficit;
- Feasibility of drastically reducing or altering services; and
- Alternative ways to balance the budget.

Case Sampler #7

Short Problem-Solving Cases with Closed Alternatives

This case is one that lends itself to group activity in the class. The alternatives are clearly presented and so permit the weighing of alternative options and presenting arguments for and against. Inherent in the arguments will be public sector values about how services should be delivered. Further, there are cost considerations as well as mitigating factors associated with the costs. Finally, there are risks inherent in each decision that can be brought forward.

TO CONTRACT OR NOT TO CONTRACT

Scenario

You are the Director of Client Service for the City of Blonk region of a provincial ministry. Your offices occupy the entire building at 56 Squish Road. As part of your duties, you are responsible for administrative and accommodation services as well as your "normal" duties of serving members of the public. Your largest service centre is on the main floor of the building.

In the past, janitorial services for the office building have been provided for employees of your department. You have become aware that many government and private sector organizations have outsourced their building maintenance.

You are now considering doing the same thing, that is, contracting for this service. You are thinking of doing this for many reasons:

- Labour costs are rising as a result of provincewide collective agreements.
- Quality of service is uneven, and so you are often fielding complaints from staff about office cleanliness and from the public about the state of the service centre.

This case originated with Dr. David Seigel, Brock University, and was adapted by Andrew Graham for instruction at Queen's University.

- The union presence is strong and takes up a lot of your time. In fact, this is your "problem group" with a large number of grievances coming from them as well as many work-related injuries leading to absences and overtime costs.
- You have begun budget planning and have been encouraged by regional office finance people to consider taking this cost "off budget" to show a net reduction in costs; you will still be spending the money, but not on staff. In other words, you are being encouraged to find ways to reduce staff complement, especially permanent staff.

You are not in the office cleaning and maintenance business. You have a large service organization with a large staff and a high degree of client interaction. That is your personal and professional focus. There is a large service centre in your building with high public traffic. You want to ensure a positive environment for both staff and clients. Ideally, you would love it if someone took this problem off your hands, just as long as you get what you want: a clean and healthy work environment with efficient and friendly public spaces.

You have just begun to look around. You contact a friend in a similar situation. She works with another ministry that has fully outsourced building maintenance. She is an enthusiastic supporter of this approach, although she warns that you will probably realize little savings. She also advises that her ministry experienced pretty strong union push back as it saw this as full-time unionized jobs going out the window.

You have two proposals from outsiders, and of course you could always continue using your own employees. Your planning horizon is five years. This means that you will have to enter into a five-year contract with the outside company if that is what you choose to do.

The Options Before You

Alternative 1: Keep Your Own Staff

Currently, you have staff being paid $500,000 per year to do this work. You have already decided that as a result of financial restraint and the need to reallocate, you will reduce that by 10 percent beginning next year. That will mean some one-time severance costs, based on the number of staff who are let go. This might be managed through voluntary retirements.

Alternative 2: ABC International Cleaners

ABC is a major international player on the office maintenance scene. It is a Boston-based company with huge operations across the United States. It has a good reputation for quality and cost control. If it gets this contract, it would be its first venture in Canada. In its terms, this is a small contract, but would establish a footing in a new market. Other maintenance firms based in Canada may react and demand that you go to competitive bidding rather than using sole sourcing.

It will do the work for $385,000 per year. Your human resources department has advised you that you will have to make one-time severance payments to laid-off employees in the amount of $300,000 in the first year of this arrangement. ABC has indicated some preparedness to consider employing some or all of the current employees but will not commit until it reviews each employee's abilities and performance.

Because ABC is new to the country and relatively unknown here, your legal department has advised you to ask for a performance bond of $100,000 to be paid upon signing of the contract. This money would be held by the department and returned without interest after five years. You would receive no benefit from the interest as it would go into the consolidated revenue of the government. ABC claims this would violate the terms of the NAFTA agreement, but has not put up strong opposition. It wants a toehold in Canada and sees this as a great opportunity to get it.

Alternative 3: Adanac Cleaners

This is a new not-for-profit company formed by a group of local Acadian and native women with some government economic development funds to enhance employment. It has been formed for the sole purpose of this contract and has no experience in either building maintenance or managing a company. Because your government has special provisions for contracting with native entrepreneurs, your choice of this group would be facilitated in terms of approvals. You would also look good in meeting a ministerial objective to improve native contracting. However, all the money for the contract would come from your existing budget. You have no track record to go on here.

Adanac will do the work for $440,000 per annum. If successful, it will take on some of your employees, probably reducing your severance payout to $50,000.

Adanac has asked that you turn over existing cleaning equipment, valued at a purchase price of $250,000 (no depreciation applied, some equipment up to ten years old). To do this you will have to find the means to "give it away" to a contractor. ABC would object to this provision. It does not want the equipment, but would press this issue as creating an unfair advantage. The cost of ABC's equipment and supply use is factored into its offer.

Your Boss Weighs In

You have not made any decision since the process has not become totally formal. However, your regional director has called and said that she is being challenged on your plans by both the regional union vice-president and the Minister's office. You have the good fortune of working in the Minister's riding, and she has received representations from all three groups you are considering.

You make it clear to your boss that nothing has been finalized. Given the political sensitivity, your boss asked that she be kept informed of

- How you are going to go about making the final decision
- How you are going make this a fair process, given the various interests and potentially human resource and legal problems at play
- The timing so that she has a "heads up"
- The probable reaction of interested groups who do not win the contract and what you suggest be done about it

In principle, the regional director is supportive of you and agrees with your rationale for considering outsourcing. But she is concerned about the union and political ramifications.

Your preliminary look at the numbers tells you that the various options are, in the final analysis, a "wash"; over the five years, overall cost differentials are similar. Of course, that does not factor in the time you and your managers now spend on building maintenance issues. Nor does it factor in the potential costs of administering a contract. As well, costs for pensions and benefits of permanent staff (not in your budget) are not factored in. Nonetheless, you want to move ahead, if only to clarify the options. You reflect that you have a number of reasons for doing this and want to be satisfied that you have considered all of these. You do want the status quo to change.

Challenge and Questions

By now, most parties are aware that you are considering options. You have not committed to any one course of action, except to gather information. But, by doing so, a dynamic is now underway and expectations and apprehensions have been created.

1. What are the merits and problems with going the contracting route versus retaining in-house services?
2. What external control factors need to be considered here? Who is in play and what are their interests? What are your risks? Who are the stakeholders?
3. What decision style is appropriate in this case?
4. What actions, in the form of a process, would you take?
5. What are the key decision factors that, based on the information available, you would have to balance in making the final decision?
6. How would you implement this decision? Who needs to be informed? When and how?

Case Sampler #8

Complex Case with Teaching Note: The Vancouver Agreement

The following case is based on a real situation. It can readily be used in the context of organizational learning or the sharing of actual practice. It is also a very good teaching case, as it is based on the notion of intergovernmental collaboration, a demanding and relevant subject for public administration virtually anywhere. A teaching note is attached as an example.

CASE STUDY: THE VANCOUVER AGREEMENT

Case Background

The Vancouver Agreement is an urban development compact among the governments of Canada, British Columbia, and the City of Vancouver. It was signed in March 2000 for a five-year term, renewed in April 2005 for a further five years, and not subsequently renewed. It has been recognized as a leading example of successful collaboration in urban governance and intergovernmental cooperation. It received an award for innovative management from the Institute of Public Administration of Canada; a United Nations public service award for improving transparency, accountability, and responsiveness in the public service; and a Partnership Award from the Association of Professional Executives of the Public Service of Canada.

This multigovernment agreement focused on improving services and making improvements to the Downtown Eastside (DTES) of the City of Vancouver, an area plagued by profound social, drug, and crime challenges. This case study reviews the process of creation of the agreement and its operations over its life. The objective of the case study is to provide contextual background for the study of public policy and management issues that include, among others

---

This case was written by the author as part of the Canada-Brazil Governance Capacity Project of the federal government of Canada and the Government of Brazil. It is unpublished to this point and used with the permission of the author.

- Intergovernmental cooperation
- Management of complex agreements
- Governance of a collaborative enterprise
- Negotiations
- Social policy

The case is also illustrative for practitioners in public policy and management in terms of the lessons learned in this complex and demanding environment about the creation of useful governance mechanisms, the process of political and bureaucratic engagement, and sustaining an initiative through transitions of government and changing priorities over time.

Source Material

Much of the material in this case has been provided by the Secretariat of the Vancouver Agreement (VA) and is available on its website at http://www.vancouveragreement.ca/. This has been supplemented through interviews with a number of individuals involved in administering the agreement. The material from these sources is organized into a case study format; this is not original research, but an assembly of existing material. Because of the richness of documentation, additional references are included at the end of this case to permit students to explore specific areas.

Origins of the Agreement

The Downtown Eastside was Vancouver's first settlement and includes the neighbourhoods of Strathcona, Chinatown, Gastown, Victory Square, and Oppenheimer/Japantown.

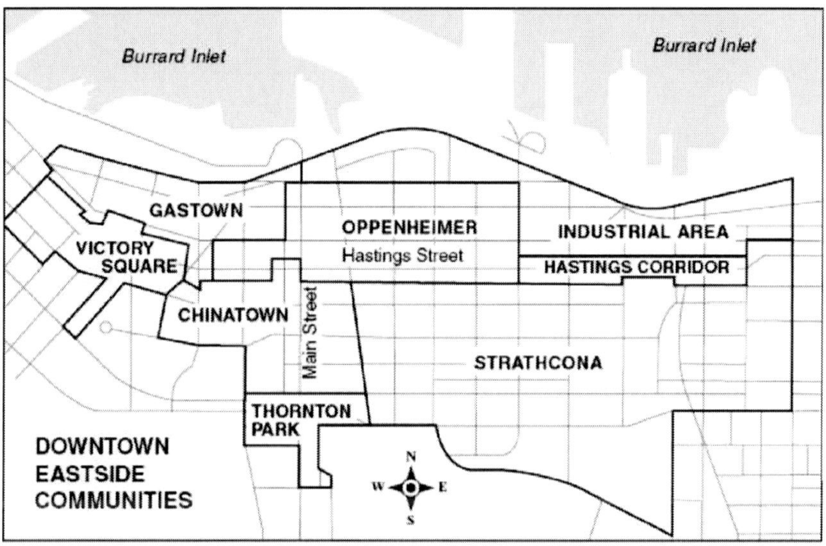

The area was once a vibrant section of the city with head offices, banks, theatres, hotels, department stores, a library, and housing for people of low and moderate incomes. The gradual loss of low-income housing in other parts of the city and the deinstitutionalization of thousands of psychiatric patients drove more people to the Downtown Eastside for affordable housing.

In the early 1990s, as the drug situation in Vancouver worsened, more people with addictions came into the community, making it a centre for drug dealing and related crimes. This affected the entire community, with a significant impact on local businesses. At the same time, large retailers and major public services were relocating toward Granville Street, the new downtown centre. Despite these changes, established residents maintained vibrant core neighbourhoods.

In the late 1990s the general perception of the DTES as a crisis zone threw into relief years of enduring policy failure and political neglect. Within the city council, efforts were already underway to integrate service delivery at the neighbourhood level throughout Vancouver. Downtown Eastside planners argued that such policy coordination between city departments would be inadequate for this neighbourhood without the active involvement of relevant provincial and federal agencies. Philip Owen, the mayor at the time, devoted considerable political energy to forging a wide-ranging partnership of governmental and non-governmental organizations to address drug addiction and criminal disorder in Vancouver, particularly the Downtown Eastside.

The immediate catalyst for the Vancouver Agreement was an acute health crisis in the Downtown Eastside – a high incidence of mental illness, drug addiction, and HIV/ AIDS within the local population. Health authorities pinpointed the Downtown Eastside as the centre of an HIV epidemic in the region.

In 1998, the City of Vancouver approved a Program of Strategic Actions for the Downtown Eastside to address the issues of crime, safety, poverty, substance abuse, homelessness, health, and economic revitalization. A five-year comprehensive DTES Revitalization Program was begun with the goal to "create a safe and healthy community." This plan had the backing of a coalition of local organizations, advocacy groups, front-line providers of services from all levels of governments, and many citizens.

Eager to institutionalize the fresh collaboration set in play by the coalition, Mayor Owen sought a politically sustainable platform to underpin it – one that would strategically bind both the provincial and federal governments, both of whom had specific jurisdictional responsibilities in this area.

It is not surprising, therefore, that in discussions on Vancouver's drug problems between the mayor's office and the federal government's Health Canada staff, urban development agreements were soon identified as a promising governance model. Such agreements have a number of characteristics:

- Horizontal integration or cooperation among governments and non-governmental agencies
- A long-term governance model
- Focus on economic and social issues in a specific area or jurisdiction
- Commitment to a continuing process of problem solving or policy focus

Urban development agreements, in various forms to suit the particular situation, exist in Winnipeg, Saskatoon, and Regina as well as in Vancouver.

It is important to note that the City of Vancouver did not have the jurisdiction or funding to fully address the complex, systemic, social and economic problems associated with the Downtown Eastside. As jurisdiction, expertise, and funding were disbursed among three levels of governments and their various agencies, participation from all levels of government was required.

The protracted writing of the Vancouver Agreement attests to the complex negotiations necessary to draw in numerous public agencies from three jurisdictional levels. A significant factor in such efforts is the challenge of coordination within the partner entities. At the outset, there were 12 federal departments, 19 provincial ministries or agencies, and 14 municipal departments having some form of responsibility in addressing the problems of the DTES including the Vancouver School Board and the Vancouver Coastal Health Authority. At the same time, it was estimated that some 300 community organizations were active in the DTES. Project participants noted that this phase and the initial start-up were periods of great vulnerability. As one observer stated, "In order to get something going, you need at least one person totally dedicated to making this happen." In this instance, the Mayor and the city CAO along with the federal government's assistant deputy minister for Western Diversification played that key binding role, bringing along the less converted, reluctant, or marginally engaged.

A draft Vancouver Agreement was endorsed by all three governments in July 1999, and received positive feedback in a community review process that then took place in the Downtown Eastside. It was formally signed in March 2000.

The Initial Agreement

The intention of the agreement was to build a collaborative effort to address a unique and demanding situation in the Downtown Eastside. As such, there was no objective to create a new level of governmental agency. All governments retained their autonomy. The agreement project itself was not to have independent funding, but rather was to be a mechanism for focusing efforts and resources. That changed in 2003 with the infusion of project-controlled funding.

In terms of how the governments organized to participate, the City was perhaps better equipped than the other levels of government. It had a Community Services Group that provided a logical organizational focus within the City. The federal and provincial governments had to create special-purpose bodies for the agreement. At the federal level, however, the Department of Western Diversification, a small federal regional development ministry with explicit coordination functions, was able to provide a platform for collaboration.

Responsibility for decisions made under the agreement rests with a Policy Committee comprising the federal Minister of Western Economic Diversification, the provincial Minister of Community, Aboriginal and Women's Services, and the Mayor of Vancouver. It proved difficult to schedule meetings to guarantee attendance of all three, so in practice the Policy Committee has met no more than twice a year, delegating strategic guidance and implementation responsibilities to a Management Committee consisting of three senior representatives from each level of government.

Despite substantial differences in jurisdictional authority and financial capacity, a decision rule of unanimous consent ensures that each governmental partner exercises equal power on the two committees. The primary operational committee of the Vancouver Agreement is a Coordination Team, which meets bi-weekly and liaises in turn with a series of task teams addressing strategic goals specified by the Management Committee. The Coordination Team also fostered the creation of and met regularly with a series of problem-focused Task Teams such as Harm Reduction, Housing, Women, Food Security, and Aboriginals that worked on street-level implementation. Task teams were not empowered to make decisions and had no funds. They had to feed into existing structures, and ministries retained full control. This created what one interviewee called "committees of second-guessing," focused on trying to scope out what might be possible within existing programming.

The strategic areas of focus for the agreement were health, economic development, safety, and housing.

Dynamics of Collaboration

Once the agreement was signed, some time was lost in launching both the governance and action elements. Very little was done to establish the working dynamic of the governance model outlined above. In fact, for the first period, informality reigned. No minutes were recorded at meetings, and decision follow-up was left to the constituent membership. As such, moving forward took both time and considerable energy. One participant noted, "We could have tied down basic processes better."

It was not until 2002 that the various governments were able to agree on a strategic plan. Many viewed this delay as a loss of potential and dynamic in the process. Others saw it as a necessary sorting out of roles.

In terms of the political dynamics surrounding the agreement, Mayor Owen, central to the earlier municipal activity, was defeated in 2002. While the agreement lost one of its original champions, his successor, Mayor Larry Campbell, was equally committed to the four pillars philosophy to ending drug abuse (prohibition, legalization, medicalization, and hard reduction) and the VA process (Collin, 2006). At the senior administrative level, city manager Judy Rogers was also a strong supporter. At the provincial level, the change in 2001 from the New Democratic Party, where the Minister of Community, Aboriginal and Women's Services had embraced the Vancouver Agreement, to the Gordon Campbell Liberal government, with its cost-cutting and business rather community development agenda, was more challenging. However, the province remained at the VA table, and indeed made the first funding move in 2003. At the federal level, the VA was actively supported by the minister responsible for Western Economic Diversification, Stephen Owen, Health minister Alan Rock, and Vancouver MP and federal secretary of state for Multiculturalism and the Status of Women, Hedy Fry. Enthusiasm waned with the election of the Conservative government in 2006, although the federal departments remained engaged. The decision not to renew the agreement for another term may well be a reflection of that government's philosophy.

Initially unfunded, the Vancouver Agreement was meant to align existing government spending, policies, and programs in the DTES. Staff and other organizational resources were released by each government to support VA activities. The premise was that policy value could be added through coordination of effort – greater focus, more seamless supports, and better knowledge. In the words of the Vancouver city manager, Judy Rogers, the "mandates of the governments differ, but are in effect complementary and are directed at the same people" (Rogers, 2001). Leadership in this coordination came from the municipality as it already had in place the Integrated Neighbourhood Service Teams. The federal and provincial governments each had greater internal challenges in bringing horizontal coherence to their own interventions before they could align with one another and the City's comparatively advanced service delivery framework (Bakvis and Juillet, 2004).

The VA's unfunded status was viewed by some as an advantage – at least at the outset – since it ensured that governmental conflict over funding, or community competition for such funding, would not deflect from the prior need to build capacities for effective spending (Macleod Institute, 2004).

Vancouver city manager Judy Rogers believed that the "value of the intergovernmental relationships cannot be overemphasized" (Rogers, 2001). The benefits identified by Rogers included mutual learning about internal systems and cultures; bringing down barriers to relationships such as that between the City and the federal government; acknowledging that issues required tri-level action and specification of where the different governments can contribute; and increasing citizen access to programs and services.

For others, however, the lack of dedicated funding soon became a hindrance to substantive progress. Existing programs and funds had conditions or rules disconnected from the complexity of needs presenting in the DTES (Bakvis and Juillet, 2004). Rogers (2001) acknowledged such limits when looking ahead:

> There are a number of challenges still to be overcome. This was initially an unfunded agreement. The partners provided funding for initiatives within their own areas of jurisdiction utilizing existing funds. These funds often came with strict program criteria and little flexibility. For example, governments have funding for job training; however, traditional job training does not fit into the DTES culture. Job training in the DTES needs to address issues such as providing relevant job training to someone involved in substance misuse. While the financial support has been significant, the need for dedicated funding has been identified as critical to the success of the Vancouver Agreement. The need for dedicated staff has also been identified as critical to moving the partners' vision forward. Finally, there are challenges with the community. The expectations of the community have been raised, but often the proposals brought forward do not fit within the criteria set by governmental programs.

In light of such concerns, the provincial and federal governments in April 2003 decided to fund specific projects initiated through the VA with a shared $20 million allocation. The catalyst was Vancouver's bid for the 2010 Olympic and Paralympic Winter Games. Conditions in the DTES represented a potential international embarrassment for the host city. On the other hand, connecting a revitalized DTES to the Olympics could help position Vancouver's bid in a wider frame of social sustainability that addressed widespread concern revealed in city consultations that the event would exacerbate urban inequalities by diverting expenditures.

With the $20 million secured, the VA partners created an Integrated Strategic Plan with four priorities. Each of these priorities reveals some unorthodox policy collaborations (Donovan and Au, n.d.; Macleod Institute, 2004; Vancouver Agreement, 2007b).

The first strategy was to revitalize the Hastings Street corridor through a combination of community economic development and public realm improvements. In partnership with the community organizations, plans were implemented to extend economic opportunity to residents through a social purchasing portal that would link businesses and governments to suppliers either based in the Downtown Eastside or who employed inner-city residents to provide goods and services. Both the 2006 World Urban Forum held in Vancouver and especially the 2010 Olympic bid presented vehicles for such a strategy. Here the VA pushed the Olympic committee to make social inclusion a key theme of the games. It commissioned a major study of potential Olympic impacts on the DTES, examining issues such as housing, business development, employment, and training. The result was the Inner City Inclusiveness Commitment in the successful Olympic bid "to promote social and economic sustainability by fully integrating the Downtown Eastside into this major international event" (Vancouver Agreement, 2007b). In addition to the $20 million from governments, the Inner City Inclusiveness Commitment was extended in 2005 when the Vancouver organizing committee announced a new partnership with Bell Canada to invest $2 million in the DTES. The money was to flow over four years to priorities identified in the VA Economic Revitalization Plan.

The second strategy was to dismantle the open drug scene in the DTES. The Safe/Supervised Injection Site was opened in 2003 under the VA's auspices. The focus was on harm reduction, moving intravenous users from the back alleys to a safe facility with access to health professionals for methadone treatment and withdrawal management services for both adults and youth. The VA mobilized the key players and facilitated relationships. Health Canada granted the responsible Vancouver Coastal Health Authority a three-year operating exemption under federal drug legislation and funded project research. The provincial Health Ministry provided funding to renovate the space and operate the site. City police were redeployed from elsewhere to ensure safety and order in the immediate area. More broadly, a coordinated prevention and enforcement strategy to end the illegal drug business "infrastructure" drew together policing, licensing, employment standards and taxation, and sentencing resources from the governments (Mason, 2006).

The third strategy was to rehabilitate rundown hotels where single occupancy rooms (SROs) had become last resort housing in the DTES. The goal of the VA's Housing Task Team was adequate housing for residents, which in turn would ease access to mental health and substance abuse services. Through the Vancouver Agreement, the City passed a by-law for renovation of SROs taking into account the housing needs of low-income residents. A pilot project with federal Canada Mortgage Housing Corporation funding provided management training for hotel staff (delivered with a community agency and community college) in dealing with SRO clientele. The conversion of the Pennsylvania Hotel was a partnership combining federal homelessness and provincial housing funding for purchase and renovation, and municipal approvals for zoning community and retail space on the bottom floor. The VA's initiative set the stage for a 2006 announcement that the three governments would undertake a $2.4-million conversion for a 44-unit housing development for low-income single people at risk of becoming homeless.

The fourth strategy was to make the community safer and healthier for the most vulnerable people in the DTES. Notable here was the collaboration for a Mobile Access Project for Sex Trade Workers. A converted ambulance vehicle made available safe spaces, first aid, peer counselling, and service referral information to sex trade workers, many of whom are vulnerable aboriginal youth. The project was led by the provincial Ministry of Community, Aboriginal and Women's Services. It worked closely with two community organizations and current and former sex trade workers who received training in front-line services. The federal Justice Department provided support in dealing with the sexual exploitation of aboriginal youth. The Vancouver Police contributed its own form of harm reduction, offering self-defence for sex trade workers and enhanced intelligence gathering on sex trade consumers. Another initiative to assist vulnerable residents came through VA support for a multiservice centre in the DTES, known as Crabtree Corner, which housed the innovative Sheway program offering support to pregnant women with substance use problems, and single mothers and their children.

Clearly, all four of the VA projects involved noteworthy collaborations not just among the three governments but also between government and the community sector, and in some cases government and business. One nonprofit executive director remarked at a 2004 awards ceremony recognizing the VA that the Urban Development Agreement was "transforming how government traditionally worked with community groups." Certainly, talk of community engagement and resident participation dated back to the VA's origins. "Community capacity building" was one of the three original themes of the VA. In the words of a Vancouver city manager:

> The importance of community input has been entrenched by the partners into the Vancouver Agreement. The capacity building approach is based on a philosophy adopted by senior governments to provide resources and support to vulnerable and marginalized communities. The goal is to assist members of the community to develop the skills, knowledge and ability to enable them to participate in the planning and decision-making process. (Rogers, 2001)

The Role of the Community

Yet, evaluations and reflections on the VA's workings suggested ongoing ambiguity surrounding the community's role. Community-based organizations were actively engaged through the VA's various task teams, but the Policy and Management Committees had not followed through on plans to include community voices in decision-making. A major evaluation of the VA reported that the governance structure did "not reflect an inclusive, integral approach that some community groups may expect" (Macleod Institute, 2004).

Outstanding issues included creating a formal policy advisory role for the community sector, supporting community capacity building and low-income resident participation, and finding ways to provide more transparent and faster access through the government bureaucracy. Moreover, the DTES "community" was itself very complex, and there were differences among interests such as Chinese merchants, aboriginal leaders, and some resident groups on issues like harm reduction (Donovan and Au, n.d.). Finding the community voice on the VA's strategic priorities was not straightforward, and longstanding distrust of government motivations was hard to overcome.

The City made the case that community representation in the DTES was handled properly through the parallel development project funded by the National Crime Prevention Centre and focused explicitly on grassroots mobilization and capacity building. Indeed, the Downtown Eastside Community Development Program (DTESCDP) represented an important learning opportunity for the VA as it engaged the community in its four projects. However, the relationship between that project and the VA was not clear, and the many lessons learned about government-community relations and engagement in the DTESCDP were not necessarily transferred to the VA (Riano-Alcalá, 2004). As the VA evaluation study summarized, "Defining what community participation means in the context of VA governance remains a piece of unfinished business" (Macleod Institute, 2004).

Outcomes

The VA has been widely recognized for developing innovative approaches to urban governance and policy, as noted at the outset of the case. As with any major policy and intergovernmental undertaking, however, issues arise for both correction and consideration.

Investment or Cooperation?

The VA's initial unfunded status reflects the fact that it was not intended to be a vehicle for large-scale redevelopment projects. Even when new money came in 2003, the amount was not sufficient for a physical, economic, or social transformation of the DTES. As such, the VA's main contributions reside in the other categories – integrating and realigning existing policies, and using modest funding across a range of partnerships for demonstrations or pilots that merit scaling-up and institutionalization.

Policy Adaptation

Through its collaborations, the VA managed to evolve a framework that clarified and better coordinated a "policy division of labour" in the DTES whereby each government delivered on its particular strength or capacity whether finances, regulation, knowledge, or convening. As Judy Rogers put it, "While the federal government was dealing with drug issues from the justice perspective, Vancouver from enforcement (policing), and the province from health (treatment), a coordinated effort on drug efforts would be more effective" (Rogers, 2001).

A survey of officials from the three levels of government found that nearly three quarters of respondents had "very often" changed their work based on lessons learned from collaborative efforts (Macleod Institute, 2004). Such government joining-up – respectful of one another's core business and open to mutual learning – informed many of the initiatives launched through the 2003 Integrated Strategic Plan. With modest funding, the VA pushed beyond existing program and policy criteria to pursue strategies more tailored to the unique conditions in the DTES. This dynamic was most evident in the exemptions to drug laws that facilitated the Safe Injection Site. It was also expressed in other initiatives: the VA's hotel conversions engaged the City in considering adding the SRO Management Course to licensing regulations; the VA's economic revitalization plans informed the social inclusion theme that became part of Vancouver's Olympic bid; and the MAP saw the Vancouver Police introduce harm reduction strategies in controlling the sex trade.

In spite of such advances, substantive challenges remained in precisely how mainstream social and economic policies affected the DTES and related to VA processes. It is clear that the factors converging to produce a DTES crisis by the late 1990s were driven by that decade's massive provincial and federal social policy cutbacks and restructurings in key fields such as social assistance, affordable housing, and mental health services. Here the VA's micro projects often were swimming against a hostile macro-policy tide. The VA's SRO conversions, for example, were a limited response to the triple threat of gentrification, development, and displacement bearing down on the DTES in the context of Vancouver's overheated housing and commercial markets. Further, some of the notable VA-sponsored successes – the inclusionary Olympic bid and the Safe Injection Site – were put in jeopardy in 2005 and 2006, when partisan government change at both the city and federal levels pushed social inclusion goals off the priority list. In fact, the political realignments were such that the VA's continued existence became an open question.

Leveraging Innovations

Here, the VA's contributions fall into several categories. First, at a broad policy level, its four-pillars framework represented a new way to conceptualize links between public health and neighbourhood revitalization. Its projects applied the principles of prevention, treatment, enforcement, and harm reduction to community development. The result was a promising policy regeneration framework with application to rundown neighbourhoods beyond the DTES. Second, in terms of specific initiatives, the Safe Injection Site piloted through the VA has drawn worldwide attention and contributed to a reframing of policy debates about substance abuse and social exclusion. Third, the VA became a model for the federal government in its New Deal for Cities and Communities. The minister, John Godfrey, frequently praised the collaboration and supported its application in other cities and to urban challenges beyond neighbourhood revitalization (Bradford, 2005). In 2005, new urban development agreements were signed in Regina and Victoria, and negotiations were underway in Toronto.

THE VANCOUVER CASE: TEACHING NOTE

Issues and Lessons Learned

This discussion of issues and lessons learned could be included either in the case or in the teaching note, depending on how the case is used. If it is used for class teaching, the lessons learned should not be in the case, but rather extrapolated in class discussion. In that sense, the lessons below are illustrative, and class participants may identify others. If the case is being used for the purposes of informing others in the context of organizational learning or knowledge transfer, the lessons learned should be included in the case.

With all its recognition and clear achievements, no collaborative effort is without both missteps and lessons learned, at least retrospectively. Further, other questions remain open for debate. The following is one possible list. Case readers and users may well find and adapt others.

1. *To fund or not to fund.* It is clear that, once the federal and provincial governments decided to dedicate funding to the Vancouver Agreement, the dynamic changed within the collaboration. It moved from being a coordinated effort of players to one in which specific resources had to be managed against a set of demands. Such processes then informed internal dynamics and also created external expectations beyond efforts at cooperation. The extent to which these dynamics can assist or hinder collaboration is a matter to consider. As one interviewee noted, "As soon as you have money, things change. You become a granting agency. You fill a vacuum with bureaucracy" (personal communication, 2009).

2. *Leadership.* The City of Vancouver provided much of the initial political and bureaucratic leadership for this initiative. It also provided staff with an ongoing commitment to the process. However, the federal government, through Health Canada and Western Diversification, also provided initial leadership. It is clear that, by 2003, the province was also committed, with the initial funding. The challenge in enterprises such as this is to survive

changes in leadership and political philosophy. One element to be noted in this almost decade-long process is that, as governments shifted, they all remained at the table in spite of these changes. They may not have been as dynamic as before, but they did not leave.

3. *Internal dynamics of collaboration or leadership from the middle.* Interviews by the author as well as the findings of other studies (Maclead Institute, 2004; Mason, 2006) confirm that an essential element of continuity is the creation of sound and positive relationships at the staff level. These are often seen as the glue that binds people together. They can also be seen as the basis for a culture of collaboration. As one long-term participant said, "I was forced to learn how other people think and what they were trying to do." Such a dynamic helps collaborative efforts get through change and also facilitates problem solving.

4. *Quality of governance.* The first years of the Vancouver Agreement were problematic from a governance perspective. There appeared to be no sense of urgency around developing the necessary planning instruments. Further, it appears to have been an issue of commitment of specific funding. While a governance structure was in place, it was not robust, especially at the Policy Committee level. Further, there was an ambiguous relationship with community players, even in light of the extensive commitment to community engagement.

5. *Accountability.* The VA was clearly committed to a collaborative process, but its commitment to accountability was less clear. Arriving at an understanding about accountability was described as "tricky" by several of the long-term participants in the agreement. The issue that the VA raises is the degree to which firm accountability really needs to be defined without detracting from the organic process of collaboration. In this instance, no autonomous program or agency was created. Therefore, the accountabilities in existence at the three levels of government were still intact. It is not always the case that more accountability is a good thing.

6. *Answerability.* While the agreement had a positive profile, there was a tendency not to designate a government lead. Participants often resorted to a "who's on first" approach to responding to external demands from the media or interest groups. At the functional level, groups worked well together on economic development and women's issues. On the issue of health, territoriality reared its ugly head. The issue here is the degree to which spokespersons or leads need to be identified in advance. This is a key part of the governance process in collaborative work.

The Theme of Building Collaborative Partnerships

Collaborative partnerships featuring intergovernmental and/or public-private sector cooperation have been identified as a leading organizational expression of the "new urban governance" (Davies, 2002; Lowndes and Skelcher, 1998). Whether tasked with developing policy responses to complex social problems or restructuring service delivery in order to meet demanding targets, these partnerships are one response to a widely recognized need for greater coordination in public administration. Consistent with the work of Ken Kernaghan (2003, p. 61), a partnership may be defined as a formal agreement to share power with others in the pursuit of joint goals and/or benefits.

The numerous types of partnerships may be distinguished by the nature and extent of control or influence exercised by the parties to the agreement. At the more ambitious end of joint working, collaborative partnerships are those in which each partner exercises power in the decision-making process; typically, these partnerships feature a pooling of resources, consensual decision rules, and a harmonization of activities (Kernaghan, 2003, p. 62).

While area-based partnerships directed toward urban regeneration goals have received sustained academic attention, there remain competing accounts of their emergence and impact. Very broadly, these comprise, on the one hand, perspectives informed by critical political economy, which suggest new modes of urban governance reacting to the dictates of global capital and, on the other hand, approaches more preoccupied with the political contexts of partnership formation. It is the latter body of research that has generated most of the recent work on collaborative policy-making and implementation for urban revitalization. Here a further distinction is useful between urban coalition theories, centred on alliances of public and private sector actors focused on boosting local economic growth, and network governance approaches, explaining partnership working in terms of local urban institutional settings and political cultures (see the surveys by Harding, 2005; and Stewart, 2005).

Sample teaching questions to explore in this context:

- What are the structures and dynamics of "successful" collaborative partnerships for urban development or for any multiparty collaborative effort?
- What would constitute the evidence for effective policy development and/or program delivery?

The Theme of Governance

Governance has many aspects: structure, interpersonal dynamics, problem-solving protocols, decision-making criteria, capacity and abilities of leadership, forming relationships. This case illustrates many of these aspects, which can be drawn out in the discussion. In addition, in this case, governance was challenged by transition and change of both people and governments with new players coming onto the scene with different and potentially harmful agendas relative to the intent of the program.

Sample teaching questions:

- What were the formal instruments of governance in the Vancouver Agreement? Why was it necessary to have several layers? Are there advantages or disadvantages to them?
- What binds good governance as evidenced in this case, and more generally?
- What were the boundaries of governance in this case? For example, what decision-making authority did the oversight Policy Committee have and what did the constituent government retain?
- Are there reflections on how an agreement such as this can flourish but still support the autonomy of the constituent players? What is the balance?

The Theme of Citizen Engagement

This case certainly raises many questions about how to effectively engage citizens and a multiplicity of non-governmental agencies and advocates within a collaborative governmental structure. In teaching this topic, some attention needs to be paid to the nature of the central problem or issue that is the object of the agreement. The DTES was and remains a controversial and politically charged physical area with an array of social problems. Therefore, strong views will be held about solutions, their urgency, and the adequacy of responses. There is clear evidence in this case that the dynamic between the community and the VA signatories was strained at times.

Sample teaching questions:

- What does the case suggest about the scope of citizen interest in this policy area? How was it articulated – through political action, through non-governmental action, and through the actions of indirectly involved groups?
- Are there limits to citizen engagement in collaborative networks of governments?
- Are there risks associated with broadly based collaborations among governments?

The Theme of Alternative Service Delivery

The VA can be seen as an effort to find an alternative service delivery tool to address pressing economic, social, and human issues in a specific location. This search reflects efforts of governments around the world for the past two decades to find better ways to service citizens. This movement is known as Citizen-Centred Service. This case has many aspects of that effort and can readily be explored in the classroom or seminar setting.

Sample teaching questions:

- Does this case present an alternative means of service delivery in the true sense? What was different? What was a traditional approach within the agreement?
- What features of the agreement reflect alternative approaches to government and governance?
- Was this a case of delivery or policy-making, or something else?

The Theme of Accountability

Accountability is a complex area of discussion, especially in the context of this case. While methods and mechanisms to account for "horizontal management" initiatives may be found in all jurisdictions, the federal Auditor General of Canada has identified three kinds of accountability required from partnering arrangements:

- Vertical accountability within each jurisdiction
- Internal accountability among the partners
- Horizontal accountability from parties involved to the public and the affected communities of interest (Desautels, 1999)

This case has elements of all three.

Sample teaching questions:

- What was the relationship of the VA to the traditional lines of governmental accountability in this case?
- Can governments alter or transfer accountabilities in their collaborative undertakings? How?
- How can governments successfully collaborate but also ensure that citizens understand who is accountable for what?

References

Bakvis, H., and L. Juillet. 2004. *The Horizontal Challenge: Line Departments, Central Agencies and Leadership*. Ottawa: Canada School of Public Service.

Bradford, N. 2005. *Place-Based Public Policy: Towards a New Urban and Community Agenda for Canada*. Research Report F|51. Ottawa: Canadian Policy Research Networks.

Collin, C. 2006. *Substance Abuse Issues and Public Policy In Canada: I. Canada's Federal Drug Strategy*. Political and Social Affairs Division, April 13. Available at http://www2.parl.gc.ca/content/lop/researchpublications/prb0615-e.html#key.

Davies, J. S. 2002. "The Governance of Urban Regeneration: A Critique of the 'Governing without Government' Thesis." *Public Administration 80*(2): 301-22.

Desautels, L. D. 1999. "Accountability for Alternative Service Delivery Arrangements in the Federal Government: Some Consequences of Sharing the Business of Government." In *Collaborative Government: Is There a Canadian Way?* eds. S. Delacourt and D. G. Lenihan. Toronto: Institute of Public Administration Canada.

Donovan, E., and W. Au. n.d. "The Vancouver Agreement, Moving Ideas Forward Together."

Harding, A. 2005. "Governance and Socio-economic Change in Cities." In *Changing Cities: Rethinking Urban Competitiveness, Cohesion and Governance,* eds. N. Buck, I. Gordon, A. Harding, and I. Turok, 62-77. Basingstoke: Palgrave Macmillan.

Institute for Citizen-Centred Service. May 2003. *Integrated Service Delivery: A Critical Analysis*. http://www.iccs-isac.org/en/publications/prdl.htm.

Kernaghan, K. 1993. "Partnerships and Public Administration: Conceptual and Practical Considerations." *Canadian Public Administration* 36(1): 57-76.

Lowndes, V., and C. Skelcher. 1998. "The Dynamics of Multi-organisational Partnerships: An Analysis of Changing Modes of Governance." *Public Administration* 76(2): 313-34.

Macleod Institute. 2004. *In the Spirit of the Vancouver Agreement: A Governance Case Study.* Calgary: University of Calgary.

Mason, M. 2006. "Collaborative Partnerships for Urban Development: A Study of the Vancouver Agreement." Department of Geography and Environment, London School of Economics, March 7.

Riano-Alcalá, P. 2004. *Communities, Community Workers and Local Government.* School of Social Work and Family Studies, University of British Columbia, August. Available at http://vancouver.ca/commsvcs/planning/dtes/pdf/DTESCDP.pdf.

Rogers, J. 2001. "Governments in Progress." Panel presentation to the FEM symposium on Cities in an Urban Century.

Stewart, M. 2005. "Collaboration in Multi-Actor Governance." In *Urban Governance and Democracy: Leadership and Community Involvement*, eds. M. Haus, H. Heinelt, and M. Stewart, 149-167. London: Routledge.

Vancouver Agreement. 2007a. "The Agreement." http://www.vancouveragreement.ca/TheAgreement.htm.

Vancouver Agreement. 2007b. "2000 2005: Progress and Highlights." http:// www.vancouveragreement.ca/Pdfs/061031FirstFiveYearsFINAL.pdf.

Case Sampler #9

Complex Case with Teaching Note: The Air Transport Case

The following case is a very good example of the kind of case that can be used by organizations to examine how one country responded to a series of challenges or by teaching institutions for class learning.

THE AIR TRANSPORT CRISIS IN BRAZIL: 2006 AND 2007

by Amâncio Jorge de Oliveira, Janina Onuki, and Sônia Naves David Amorim

Introduction

This case study addresses the crisis that befell the Brazilian air transport sector in 2006 and 2007 and was referred to by the media as "aviation chaos" or "aviation blackout." The crisis, which was kickstarted by a major aviation accident, had as its main players the air traffic controllers who, under the suspicion of operational failure and due to their difficulties in communicating with the authorities, reacted by starting a work-to-rule protest ("white strike"). This, coupled with insufficient personnel, led to inadequate operational control in the main airports in the country from November 2006 to mid-2007, with great loss of life. A second accident during this period deepened

---

This is the second case study in a new line of research of the General Coordination of Research/Brazilian National School of Public Administration (ENAP), which was initiated in 2008 with the release of the case studies series "The Environmental Licensing for Hydroelectric Dams on the Madeira River." The objective is to consolidate the case studies as a methodology for the training of public servants with a focus on applied learning. The case was finalized in October 2009.

Amâncio Oliveira and Janina Onuki are instructors in the negotiation course offered by ENAP and professors at the Brazilian Centre for International Negotiation Studies – CAENI, at the University of São Paulo. Sônia Amorim is technical advisor of the General Research Coordination Unit, Communication and Research Board, ENAP.

the crisis, raising doubts among the Brazilian public as to the structural and professional efficiency of an area that had so far been considered safe, even by international standards.

The case reports the attempts by the authorities responsible for the air transport policy to solve the crisis vis-à-vis the discontentment and grievances of air traffic controllers and the rage of society.

The report comprises two different moments: the accident involving a GOL Airlines flight and an Embraer Legacy jet owned by an American company in September 2006, and the accident involving a TAM airplane at Congonhas Airport in São Paulo in July 2007.

The case focuses primarily on the initial stage of the crisis, especially the negotiations that took place between air traffic controllers and Brazilian government authorities. The second event in the crisis is described in the case only to justify the worsening of the situation and to clarify the context in which the negotiations with air traffic controllers took place from that moment on.

The original objective of this case study, which was written for a workshop on public sector negotiation, was to illustrate a situation of crisis and a negotiation process. However, the case could also be used on a broader scale, offering support material for public policy and public management studies addressing, *inter alia*, the following topics:

- Negotiation
- Crisis management
- Communication
- Management of public litigation matters
- Strategic planning

The Institutional Context

The institutional structure of the Brazilian aviation sector helps give an understanding of the context in which the crisis and the negotiations between air traffic controllers and Brazilian authorities developed.

Air traffic control in Brazil is run by the military sector through the Aviation Command, which is linked to the Ministry of Defence. The Ministry was created in 1999, with the mission of exercising supreme control over the Armed Forces, consisting of the Navy, the Army, and the Air Force, within the framework of a set of institutional reforms in the field of military-civilian relations, with a view to ensuring greater adjustment to the reality of the democratic regime. Since its inception, the Ministry has been headed by civilians, which has led to occasional organizational culture shocks.

The responsibility for managing the Brazilian aviation sector as a whole is shared by the Air Force Command and several institutions, of which the most important are the Brazilian Air Force (FAB), the National Civil Aviation Agency (ANAC), and the Brazilian Airport Infrastructure Company (Infraero).

ANAC's role consists of regulating and inspecting civil aviation activities. The agency was set up in 2002 to replace the Civil Aviation Authority. It is a federal regulatory agency operating under a special autocratic regime and linked to the Ministry of Defence.

It is important to qualify that even after ANAC was created, air traffic control and accident investigation activities remained within the Air Force Command and the Ministry of Defence. Regulation and inspection responsibilities involve setting flight safety standards and defining the air traffic network as well as minimum airport infrastructure conditions and economic relations within the scope of civil aviation.

Infraero, in turn, is responsible for managing the main airports in the country. With the status of a Brazilian government corporation, the company is also linked to the Ministry of Defence. Like ANAC, Infraero has no direct responsibility for air traffic control.

The direct responsibility for air traffic control belongs to the Air Force. The structure of air traffic control is carried out by units called Integrated Air Traffic Control and Air Defence Centres (Cindacta). Each of these units carries out commercial and military air traffic control activities and keeps watch over Brazilian airspace and commands the country's defence actions. The system is made up of four units: Cindacta I (Brasília), Cindacta II (Curitiba), Cindacta III (Recife), and Cindacta IV (Manaus).

A fundamental feature of the air traffic control system, which was in the eye of the crisis, is the air traffic controller, also known by the international recognized abbreviation, ATCO. The profession has not yet been regulated by the Brazilian government. The flight controllers' function is to issue and give the necessary instructions and information within the airspace in their jurisdiction in order to prevent collisions between aircraft and obstacles in the vicinity of airports.

According to a Ministry of Labour study carried out in 2007, 2,700 people were involved in this activity, a number considered insufficient to meet the country's demand.

In Brazil there are two categories of air traffic controllers: military controllers (sergeants), numbering around 2,200 (81.14 percent), and civilian controllers, totalling approximately 500 people (18.51 percent). Part of the civilian group is linked to Infraero and part is made up of civilian Air Force employees belonging to the DACTA group. The groups are governed by different legislation as to salaries and retirement rules. Civilian controllers are trained at the

Airspace Control Institute (ICEA) in São José dos Campos, and the military controllers at the Air Force Specialists School (EEAR) in Guaratinguetá. Both training centres are located in the state of São Paulo.

Origin and Development of the Crisis

The air transport crisis can be characterized as a complex event, given the multiplicity of actors involved and events that unfolded.

To put it simply, one could say that the crisis comprised seven main moments: the generating event (the 1st accident) → the institutional crisis (the air traffic controllers' "mutiny") → the harder-line position adopted by the military →negotiations (civil command) → the new event and new crisis outbreak (2nd accident) → the resumption of military control of the crisis management → and punishment and return to normality.

The First Moment of Crisis: September 2006

The crisis started in September 2006 with the collision between the Boeing 737-800 belonging to GOL Airlines, which was carrying 154 passengers, and an Embraer Legacy Executive jet, on its way to being delivered to an American client. Both were flying on the air route Brasilia-Manaus.

The crash, which led to the death of all 154 people aboard the Boeing, was the worst in the history of Brazilian aviation to that date.

During the investigations, all plausible hypotheses for why the accident had happened were considered. The main theories involved human error on the part of the American pilots; technical faults in the Legacy jet, especially failure of the transponder; communication problems between the pilots of the two aircrafts; technical faults in the air traffic control equipment; and human error on the part of the air traffic controllers.

The blame, which had initially fallen on the American pilots of the Legacy, was soon transferred to the air traffic controllers on duty at the time of the accident, drawing controllers to the centre of the crisis.[1] During the investigations, 18 air traffic controllers were temporarily removed from duty, thus overburdening those who remained at work and causing great tension among the staff.

Under pressure, the controllers reacted by leaking to the press problems related to the quality of the equipment and flight monitoring system, and complained about the treatment the class was getting from the authorities, their double affiliation (civilian and military), and unfavourable working conditions.

To manage the situation, the government established a working group that included three ministries (Finance, Defence, and Planning), the Solicitor

General's Office, the Air Force Command, the National Civil Aviation Agency, the National Flight Protection Workers' Union, the National Aviation Workers' Union, and the National Airline Union.

On October 17, 2006, the working group held its first meeting to propose solutions to the crisis. Among other suggestions, the Minister of Defence proposed the demilitarization of air traffic control as a way of resolving the deadlock.

On October 22, the air traffic controllers held a secret meeting. According to a press report (*Folha de São Paulo*, October 27, 2006), the most radical of the proposals discussed by the 60 or so professionals present concerned a strike or "work-to-rule" of civilian controllers, expressed in the form of intentional delays to flights, as a way of showing their dissatisfaction with the precarious working conditions at the time.

The Brazilian Air Force (FAB) immediately published a note denying that there had been any meeting involving professionals who were involved in air traffic control. The note also highlighted the professionalism of the military personnel operating in air traffic control and the efforts of the president of the Controllers Association to operate in partnership to overcome the crisis, refuting, therefore, any opportunist positions aimed at obtaining improved salaries or short-term demands. The main concern of the FAB note was to simultaneously show coordination and dispel any rumours of fractures in the line of command.

On October 28, air traffic controllers at Cindacta I region started a work-to-rule operation that resulted in flight delays and cancellations in the south and southeast of the country, as well as disturbances and passenger protests in the airports.

As part of the work-to-rule operation, each air traffic controller started to monitor a maximum of 14 aircrafts. This limit was in keeping with international air safety standards set by the International Air Traffic Controllers' Federation. This was, in fact, the argument used by the Brazilian International Air Traffic Controllers' Federation (Febracta) to deny that they had started a work-to-rule operation; they claimed that this measure was taken to adjust the air traffic controllers' workload to the levels established in international regulations. Febracta made a number of public announcements presenting this work-to-rule as an initiative aimed at guaranteeing the safety of the system.

The sixth day of the work-to-rule operation coincided with the eve of the All Souls Day holiday and resulted in delays of up to six hours at airports.

The President, in a meeting with his advisors, reacted strongly and asked if the country was being "held to ransom by the controllers." The meeting was attended by the Air Force Commander, the Minister of Defence, the Chief of Staff, and the presidents of Infraero and ANAC.

At this time, according to a press report, the President asked ANAC to justify its reasons for authorizing aviation companies to operate new routes, in spite of the shortage of controllers to monitor the airspace. The President also demanded an explanation from the Air Force of why it had cancelled a public investigation to hire 144 controllers, which had been set for June of that year. Finally, the President asked the Chief of Staff for information about what had happened to the Civil Aviation Council (Conac) study carried out in October 2003, which had drawn attention to the risk of a collapse in the air control system as a result of investment cutbacks in the sector.

The limit on the number of aircrafts that were being monitored was not, however, the only tactic adopted by air traffic controllers as a means of protest.

In November 2006, a group of controllers took sick leave. The Air Force Command immediately adopted a more hard-line position and decided to confine 200 air traffic control sergeants to their barracks. This confinement did not have the desired effect, and flight delays continued all over Brazil. As a result, the head of the Airspace Control Department was relieved of his post.

On November 16, after interviewing air traffic controllers, the Air Force Command released a preliminary report showing that there had been communication problems between the Legacy pilots and air traffic control. The Air Force Commander publicly admitted to human error on the part of air traffic controllers as one of the causes of the accident.

At the same time, the Federal Police started an inquiry and began to interview the air traffic controllers involved.

This tense situation dragged on through the end of 2006 and into 2007, reaching its peak on March 29, 2007, when Cindacta I (Brasília) controllers went on strike. The decision to down tools all over the country was a reaction to the warnings issued by the unit's commander, who said he would not hesitate to "use the rule book," which meant imprisonment for going on strike.[2] There were now 260 controllers confined to their barracks in Brasília, Manaus, Salvador, Curitiba, and Rio de Janeiro. This was a significant number, representing roughly 10 percent of the total number of active controllers. The controllers told their superiors that they would only authorize the landing of aircrafts that were already airborne, on emergency missions, or carrying transplant patients.

As a consequence, Infraero decided to suspend air traffic at all 49 commercial airports in Brazil.

The extension of this strike action and the absence of any short-term, viable alternatives made the entire system vulnerable and put the government in a difficult situation.

One option available to the government at the time was to hire foreign controllers. In the event of an emergency, Brazilian legislation allows public service workers to be hired without the need for a public examination, which is traditionally a very slow process. The effectiveness of this alternative was, however, questionable. According to the Aviation Workers' Union, it takes at least two months for a new hire to become *au fait* with the job. The worsening crisis would not allow for a solution that took so long to be put into practice.

The strikers had five basic demands:

1. An end to persecution and the immediate return of the association's representatives and supervisors who had been removed from their jobs
2. The creation of an emergency bonus for air traffic controllers and the development of a career plan for these workers
3. A beginning to the demilitarization process, with the voluntary absorption of the labour force working as military air traffic controllers
4. The setting up of a committee with representatives of the executive authorities and controllers (both civilian and military) to monitor the changes in Brazilian air traffic
5. Modernization of the equipment used in air traffic control

Of these demands, the most complex concerned the demilitarization of the career of air traffic controller. A statement issued by the president of the Brazilian Air Traffic Controllers' Association in November 2006 clearly showed just how unsatisfied they were with the militarization of the sector: "The controller is a sergeant who cannot earn a differentiated salary, because this would cause problems with the other sergeants. On the other hand, we have only one rung on our ladder, which is inconsistent with a military job. This career is not compatible with the military area" (*Mattedi*, November 6, 2006). This statement was categorical in its preference for civilian control of the sector.

As the situation worsened, the Minister of Defence decided to meet with aviation sector leaders, so that steps to deal with the crisis could be taken. The Minister held a press conference after the meeting, which showed that a weak, hesitant position had been assumed in view of the magnitude of the crisis. The Minister made contradictory statements about whether the government would negotiate directly with the strikers. Furthermore, the Minister was seen to have little knowledge of the technical aspects of air traffic control and did not disclose the measures that would be taken to overcome the crisis. Because of his political history as an exile during the military dictatorship, the Minister was rejected by most of the military.

The President of the Republic, who at that time was on official visit to the United States, was urged to change the approach and thus nominated the Minister of Planning, Budgeting and Management to start up direct negotiations with the controllers' representatives. For the second time, the President resorted to choosing a civilian minister to negotiate with the controllers. In November 2006, the Labour Minister had been asked to do the same.

The foundations for an agreement were laid down in a meeting with the controllers, which was also attended by the Air Force Commander and the Director of the Infraero Airspace Control Department. These negotiations had an immediate effect and the controllers decided to call off the strike. One of the agreements reached during these negotiations between the Minister and the strikers was that a meeting would be held with the President where the controllers' grievances could be aired.

The decision to negotiate directly with the controllers and to grant them substantial concessions was a calculated risk. The government ran the risk of setting a precedent and stimulating other public sector services, both inside and outside the Armed Forces, to protest in the same way. One example where this risk was apparent was the case of the Federal Police, which had gone on strike for better salaries not long before the controllers were confined to their barracks.

The negotiations between the Minister of Planning, Budgeting and Management and the controllers' representatives took place on March 30, 2007, at Cindacta I, in Brasília. The negotiators also requested the presence of the Chief of Staff, but she could not attend as she was away on an official trip. The controllers' strategy was to request the presence of authorities who had real decision-making power as a way to reinforce the guarantees that whatever was agreed would be actually implemented.

After some government concessions, an agreement was reached that put an end to the strike. In the agreement, which was signed by the Minister of Planning, Budgeting and Management and the Deputy Chief of Staff, the government committed to

1. Review all disciplinary acts, including work transfers and layoffs, so as to ensure that those involved would not be punished
2. Establish a permanent negotiation channel with the representatives of air traffic controllers, to discuss the gradual demilitarization of air traffic control in Brazil
3. Establish, in the short term, a negotiation channel to discuss issues related to the salaries of both civilian and military controllers

In addition to these three formal commitments, it was informally agreed that a meeting would be arranged between the controllers and the President of the Republic.

According to analysts, however, the agreement had no solid ground to stand upon. The weakness of the first commitment stems from the fact that the military are governed by specific disciplinary codes of their own. Given that most controllers were military, it was impossible to assure them that they would not be punished. In fact, the hybrid composition of the controllers' movement owing to the presence of both military and civilian controllers was an Achilles heel in that the potential cost was higher for military than for civilian controllers. The weaknesses of the second and third commitments were clear, in that they mentioned establishing a dialogue and negotiations but offered nothing of substance.

Despite these weaknesses, the negotiation between the Minister and the controllers was the most decisive factor in overcoming the crisis, in that the process led controllers to step back.

The other alternative would have been to arrest the controllers on charges of contempt, but this could have reignited tensions and caused the conflict to scale up, with unpredictable developments. This means that two clearly opposite strategies collided at that moment: the *coercive* strategy defended by the military command and the *persuasive* strategy defended by the President and carried out by the Minister of Planning, Budgeting and Management.

The end of the strike at Cindacta I set off a chain reaction. The other Centres (Cindactas) also went back to work. In addition to ending the strike, the controllers' decision was marked by a public manifesto of apology to Brazilian society. The Brazilian Association of Air Traffic Controllers (ABCTA), the entity representing the controllers, issued the following communiqué, which was posted on its website: "May March 30 be remembered as 'a cry for help from Air Traffic Controllers' and not a simple military rebellion. We apologize to Brazilian society and ask for peace so that we can go back to doing our job with excellence."

The persuasive line of negotiations, however, soon went sour. Shortly after a meeting with the Minister of Planning, Budgeting and Management, the President re-established military authority and announced that the negotiations would again be led by the Air Force. More specifically, the President stated that the Air Force Commander would resume control of the negotiations in place of the Minister of Planning, Budgeting and Management.

The reason for this change in position was to ensure that the Armed Forces were once again in charge of the negotiations. The Air Force Commander had threatened to resign his position as he felt his authority had been undermined due to the confusion between the military approach, with its threats of punishment, and the civil approach of negotiations and concessions. To the press, the Air Force Commander denied feeling that his authority had been undermined by the President of the Republic.

The President's decision to re-establish the military authority in negotiations with the controllers was interpreted by some organized sectors of society and the media as a breach of contract. In the opinion of these critics, the government had thrown out the agreement signed. The new context enhanced the prospects of punishment for protesting controllers, based on the Military Inquiries (IPMs) proposed by the Public Prosecutor's Office.

The approach adopted by the executive authorities was very different from that taken by the military. The latter tried to quash the strikers by threatening them with imprisonment, intimidation, and retaliation; the executive authorities, however, tried to negotiate with them directly. The President had ordered that the arrest warrants issued against the strikers by the military be revoked. Had he not done so, there was a risk that the conflict would have escalated, making it more difficult for the situation to return to normal. By re-establishing military control over the negotiations, the government agreed to the coercive approach proposed by the military.

A step back by the government was also seen with respect to the proposal to demilitarize air traffic. One of the possibilities considered would have entailed transferring, by provisional measure, 1,500 of the 2,200 military controllers to the so-called General Air Traffic Control, a civilian entity linked to the Ministry of Defence. According to the president of the ABCTA, about 90 percent of all military controllers were willing to join the civilian system; this was an important claim from controllers. However, demilitarization was a never-to-be-fulfilled promise made within the scope of the negotiations led by the Minister of Planning, Budgeting and Management.

The Brazilian Bar Association (OAB) received and accepted an ABCTA request to act as a mediator in the negotiations between controllers and the government. According to the OAB president, the association's role was not to act as the controllers' defence attorney, but rather as civil society's representative in the negotiation process.

The relationship between controllers and civil society was another sensitive issue. Controllers found themselves in a dilemma: if the idea that they had been the victims of precarious working conditions prevailed, there would be a greater chance of their being in a better bargaining position and having their grievances accepted. If their grievances were considered to be opportunistic and exaggerated, they ran the risk of turning public opinion against them and ending up in an even weaker position.

This was a very unusual situation for a sector that is considered as providing an essential public service to find itself in. The leaders needed to decide whether to call a strike or not. There was the risk that public opinion would turn against the strike and they would be unable to settle the grievances that had motivated it. On the other hand, if their grievances were met, the movement would be strengthened. Controllers also had to bear in mind that their situation was one that affected the entire country.

In fact, the air traffic controllers' movement split Brazilian public opinion. Part of society, especially the press, started to unleash strong criticisms of the movement. This case even started to induce pressure to alter the way in which strikes in essential public services are dealt with.

Some organized movements, however, adopted positions backing the air traffic controllers. One of these was the Permanent Air Safety Forum, which was up in May 2007 specifically to support the controllers. The formal filing of a public action claiming pain and suffering was one of the first steps taken by the Forum, which was made up of a number of institutions and individuals such as the São Paulo Regional Public Prosecutor's Office, the director of the São Paulo Faculty of Public Health, representatives of the Municipality of São Paulo Sanitary Watch, and the Consumer Protection Institute (Pera and Stein, 2007). Some left-wing parties, such as the United Socialist Workers Party (PSTU), also declared their support for the air traffic controllers' movement.

Just as the situation looked like it was going to stabilize, in July 2007 there was a second tragedy. The effect of this second event was to significantly intensify the crisis, as described below.

The Second Event in the Crisis: July 2007

Amid efforts to negotiate with the different segments involved, the crisis was worsened by another serious aviation accident.

On July 17, 2007, a TAM Airbus A320 coming from Porto Alegre skidded on the runway at Congonhas Airport and collided with a cargo terminal belonging to the same company, TAM Express. The total of 199 dead, including passengers, crew, and TAM Express employees, made this the worst disaster in Latin American civil aviation history. Not only did the number of victims exceed those killed in the earlier crash, but this accident had a greater impact on public opinion, as the collision occurred in the centre of a huge metropolis and was filmed and widely screened on television.

The two accidents were viewed by experts not as two separate events but rather as part of a structural, systemic problem that affected the Brazilian aviation sector. As a result, domestic public opinion began to cast serious doubts on the efficiency of the aviation sector infrastructure in the country and on the capability of the agencies responsible for managing the sector.

In this scenario, the focus switched from air traffic controllers to the Brazilian Aviation Agency (ANAC), which was blamed for being lenient throughout the crisis. The government then began to pressure the agency's directors who, by law, could not be removed from office as this would translate into government interference in an independent regulatory agency.

The Outcome

The worsening of the crisis after the second air disaster made the position of the Minister of Defence unsustainable. On July 25, 2007, he was relieved of his post in spite of his friendship with the President of the Republic. His removal from office came about for reasons that went beyond the aviation crisis. The minister had always found it difficult to deal with military commands, due to his having been banished into political exile during the military government and to certain personality traits. The military had always considered him too indecisive for the job, and the crisis had only reinforced this viewpoint.

His place was taken by a politician who was known to be a skilful negotiator and who was widely respected by Congress. His main asset was his ability to operate comfortably in different parts of the federal bureaucracy, which gave him the confidence to make decisions. His introduction started to bring peace to the situation.

Air traffic controllers were forced, especially in view of the pressure from public opinion and civil and military authorities, to tone down their demands.

The controllers' grievances were only partly met. The main demand, which was demilitarization of the sector, was put on hold for further study. The outcome showed that the controllers had lost the struggle and that the structural problems had not been fully tackled. However, if a hard-line approach had been maintained and if the President of the Republic had not made some concessions, the outcome could have been worse. Mass layoffs and imprisonment of the controllers were not out of the question. In other words, the final result lay somewhere between the worst possible scenario (layoffs) and the best (meeting the grievances).

The trials and punishment of the military controllers started in August 2007. As expected, the military group of controllers had to endure the toughest consequences of the strike. The Military Prosecutor's Office accepted the charges from regional military prosecution services. The military controllers were being accused mainly of promoting a rebellion by jointly refusing to obey their commander's orders. The crime is provided for in Article 149, Paragraph III of the Military Criminal Code. Arrests were made in Curitiba and Manaus. In other words, the coercive approach prevailed.

The main element of weakness in the air traffic controllers' movement was the hybrid composition of the staff, which included both military and civilians. The military controllers, who were subject to the military disciplinarian regime, had greater chances of being severely punished. This differential cost undermined the bargaining power of the controllers' representatives in the negotiations, to the point that they agreed to give in and end the strike as a result of the negotiations with Minister of Planning, Budgeting and Management, on the basis of very vague commitments.

Notes

[1]In the Federal Police report of May 2007, the American pilots were charged with having contributed to the accident, as they had unintentionally turned off the transponder. The Public Prosecutor's Office subsequently submitted the case to the Federal Court of the city of Sinop, in the State of Mato Grosso. In December 2008 the pilots and air traffic controllers involved were acquitted of some of the charges by the federal judge of the city of Sinop. Based on a report issued by the Centre for the Investigation and Prevention of Aviation Accidents, the Public Prosecutor's office filed an appeal in May 2009 and submitted a new lawsuit to the Federal Court including other charges, which is still pending.

[2] The context was similar to that of an air traffic controllers' strike that took place in the United States in 1981, during the Ronald Reagan government. In this case, however, the government decided to stand firm and 48 hours after the strike began, 12,000 employees were fired (Pera and Stein, 2007).

Bibliography

ANAC. 2008. *Regras e Emendas aos Regulamentos da ANAC*. Ministry of Defence. Accessed December 2, 2008, at http://www.anac.gov.br.

Andrade, T. 2007. *A crise da Varig/TAM e o uso do* code share.

Arbix, G. 2002. "Da liberalização cega dos anos 90 à construção estratégica do desenvolvimento." *Tempo Social* 14(1): 1-17.

Burle, L. L. 2003. "Transporte aéreo no Brasil: a crise da aviação civil." *Indicadores Econômicos FEE* 31(3): 5-18.

Castro, N., and L. Philippe. 1993. "Desregulamentação do setor de transporte: o subsetor transporte aéreo de passageiros." *Discussion Text* No. 319. Brasília: IPEA.

Fay, C. 2001. "Crise nas alturas: a questão da aviação civil." PhD dissertation, Porto Alegre.

Guimarães, E., and L. H. Salgado. 2003. *A regulação do mercado de aviação civil no Brasil*. Rio de Janeiro: IPEA.

Monteiro, C. F. 2008. "O 'apagão aéreo' e as relações entre Estado e Mercado." Study presented at the 6th ABCP Meeting, Campinas, UNICAMP.

Novais e Silva, L. 2008. "Tópicos sobre a evolução da aviação comercial no Brasil." Accessed November 29, 2008, at http://juas2.uol.com.br/doutrina/texto.asp?id=9133.

Oliveira, A. V. 2007. "Regulação da oferta no transporte aéreo: do comportamento de operadoras em mercados liberalizados aos atritos que emergem da interface público-privado." Working Document No. 024, São José dos Campos, Air Transport Competition and Regulation Study Centre, August.

Pêgo Filho, B. 2002. "Setor aéreo e as empresas brasileiras: situação atual e perspectivas." *IPEA Bulletin,* No. 59: 73-78.

Pera, G., and Stein, L. 2007. "Greve e complexidade, dilema do movimento dos controladores de tráfego aéreo no Brasil (2006–2007)." Study presented at the 31st ANPOCS meeting, Caxambu.

Pereira, A. 1987. *Breve história da aviação comercial brasileira*. Rio de Janeiro: Europa.

Salgado, L., and R. Motta, eds. n.d. "Regulação e concorrência no Brasil: governança, incentivos e eficiência." Rio de Janeiro: IPEA.

Teaching Note: The Air Transport Case

For the purpose of a workshop or course on public sector negotiations, the case should be analyzed in light of the following guiding questions:

- What strategies were adopted by the Brazilian authorities in their relations with air traffic controllers?
- Could more effective strategies have been adopted?
- Was there coordination among the bureaucratic Brazilian spheres in the negotiation process with air traffic controllers?
- What lessons can be drawn from this case as regards the process of planning negotiations in a situation of crisis involving a professional category in the Brazilian public administration?

The following script is suggested for simulating other possible negotiation alternatives among the actors involved in the case. The simulation is to be developed in four phases by workshop participants, who will be divided into six groups.

Phase I: Preparation and Pre-negotiation (2 hrs)

Phase I involves the preparation and pre-negotiation steps. At this point, there are no binding commitments; that is, the consultations and positions do not generate commitment for the parties. This phase should be dedicated to collecting data and mapping interests. It is divided into three activities as follows:

1. General instructions and group formation (30 min):

Instructors provide information to participants on the objectives and operation of the simulations.

Instructors should highlight two points with respect to the objectives: (i) that the simulations seek to emulate real-life situations to get participants to make intense use of the techniques learned during the workshop; and (ii) that the objectives consolidate the main negotiation concepts and theory.

It is important to point out that while the case to be simulated is based on a real-life situation in the federal public administration, participants should address it as if it were something totally new to them. In other words, they should make their own decisions rather than following those made in the actual case. The real-life case is to be used for reference purposes only.

Following presentation of the general instructions, the class is broken down into six groups:

- Air Force Command
- Ministry of Defence

- Ministry of Planning, Budgeting and Management
- Workers' Union President
- Civil society representatives
- Representative of Air Traffic Controllers

2. Reading and preparing negotiations (30 min):

The groups will be given their instructions, which contain four topics arranged on a single card (personal profile, interests, justice standards, and facts). This information will give the groups a good idea of their goals and the conditions required for achieving them.

3. Knowledge and survey of interests (1 hr):

The groups will then be allowed their first conversation with one another. This is a time for making introductions and surveying interests. At this point, the groups will convey their points of view and interests to one another in a very preliminary fashion.

Once the survey phase is completed, participants meet again with their respective group mates in order to define strategies.

The groups should complete interest-mapping forms so as to organize their interests, priorities, strengths, and weaknesses. This activity, in addition to adding to the negotiation dynamics, will help to consolidate concepts.

Phase II: Bilateral negotiations (4 hrs)

Bilateral negotiations are the starting point of formal negotiations. In this phase, contrary to what was done in the pre-negotiation phase, commitments become binding. Offers should therefore be carefully made as they generate the expectation of a formal commitment to the other party.

Instructors should provide an agenda for bilateral meetings. There is no strict order for scheduling bilateral meetings. In this particular case, bilateral meetings are recommended as a way of separating government from non-government representatives and starting negotiations using a panel system, where all groups negotiate with one another. Once the panel activity is completed, all groups start defining their own strategies for multilateral negotiations.

Phase III: Multilateral negotiations (4 hrs)

1. Multilateral Negotiations (3 hrs, 30 min):

Each group will designate a chief negotiator to participate in the multilateral negotiations. Only chief negotiators can interfere directly in the negotiation process. The other members can send messages or interact separately with their delegates. Intragroup consultations should not exceed 3 minutes.

2. Drafting the final agreement (30 min):

The agreement should be as detailed as possible. Each group representative signs the agreement, which should be drafted in the simple text format. Topics not agreed upon could be enclosed in brackets. Once signed, the topics become binding commitments.

Phase IV: Analyzing the Final Agreement: Negotiation Dynamics and Final Evaluation (4 hrs)

Instructors then make comments on the results achieved as well as on the negotiation process as a whole and the agreement signed. With respect to the agreement, comments should take into account the objectivity of the criteria, detailing of duties and rights as well as other formal aspects involved in the preparation of final agreements. As for comments on the negotiations held, instructions should focus on aspects that could be improved. At this point, it is essential that links be established between the fundamental concepts and techniques presented during the course and concrete examples provided during the simulation exercises.

Appendix: The Brazilian Civil Aviation Sector in Numbers

- In March 2008, there were 16 companies operating domestic flights and seven Brazilian operating international routes.
- There were around 11,400 registered aircraft in 2008, compared with 9,768 in 1996.
- According to Infraero, in January 2008, Brazilian airline companies carried 9.97 million people. This represents a 2.8 percent increase over the previous year.
- A Ministry of Labour study carried out in 2007 showed that there were 2,700 air traffic controllers in Brazil, a number that was considered insufficient to meet the country's growing demand for this activity. The study also reported that air traffic was expanding at a rate of around 9 percent a year, whereas new controllers were being hired a rate of no more than 3 percent a year.
- The three largest airports in Brazil are, in order of capacity: Cumbica, in Guarulhos; Galeão, in Rio de Janeiro; and Congonhas, in São Paulo.
- The two main domestic companies, namely TAM and GOL, together employ more than 50,000 people.

Sources: ANAC, Infraero, and the Ministry of Labour.

Case Sampler #10

An Organizational Learning Case: The Tale of Two Contracts

This case focuses on transferring knowledge about specific practices. It can be argued that it is as much of an article as a case. However, what happens to the main character of the story, as small a part as he plays, sets the stage for the provision of very useful and practical information.

A TALE OF TWO CONTRACTS
or, How to Minimize the Risk of Forming an Employment Contract while Acquiring Goods, Services, or Construction
by Cathryn Kallwitz

If the following story has you reaching to brush the dust off of a contract you established long ago (or perhaps more recently…), you may not be alone. Across town, your contractor might be doing the same thing, and for entirely the same reason. But, it might not have to be this way. This article looks at what procurement and employment relationships mean and what can be done to minimize or mitigate the risk of an employment relationship forming under what began as a procurement contract, both before it is signed and while the ink is still relatively fresh.

Cathryn Kallwitz is the Manager, Methodology and Standards at RFPSOLUTIONS Inc., a private sector firm based in Ottawa that works exclusively with government clients to plan and implement procurement strategies, develop written statements of work and evaluation criteria, and provide procurement-related consulting and advisory services and productivity tools. Cathryn can be reached at cathryn@rfpsolutions.ca.

This article was originally published by RFPSOLUTIONS in *FMI Journal* 20, no. 1 (Autumn 2008): 19-24, http://www.rfpsolutions.ca/articles/A_Tale_of_Two_Contracts_Cathryn_Kallwitz_FMI_Oct2008_E.pdf. Reprinted with permission.

George was well-liked by his colleagues, and had worked hard over the past ten years. From April to October every year, George worked in the field surveying and cataloguing a variety of items of interest to the department. His work began on schedule each spring, with George setting off across the country in the ministry car – not only was he able to get to each work site in a timely manner to complete the work, but the bright logos and word mark on the vehicle enhanced visibility of the ministry's mandate and activities in the communities he visited. Late one afternoon as George set off back to the car, making some final notes with his ministry pen on his logo-covered clipboard, he tripped and fell into the ravine that ran alongside the road. He was not discovered until sometime later that evening. As a result of his fall, George was unfortunately unable to continue his survey work. His partner submitted a request for long-term disability to the new manager at the ministry, and was informed that, despite years of dedicated service, George was ineligible for coverage under the public service plan. Some time ago, the ministry had established a multiyear contract with George to provide his annual surveying service. As this came as somewhat of a surprise, his partner requested a ruling on the status of George's working relationship with the ministry. Despite the existence of a signed procurement contract, based on an examination of the relationship, the investigation determined that George had been treated as, and was thus in fact, an employee. George and his partner received the much-needed benefits, and the ministry was fined for the unremitted Employment Insurance and Canada Pension Plan (plus interest) for the ten years of George's services.

The establishment of a procurement contract to support the delivery of any government program or service is a valid option to obtain the goods, services, or construction required to design, develop, implement, maintain, and/or evaluate any short-term initiative or aid in ongoing operations. Building internal capacity through staffing can be equally effective. Therefore, prior to initiating any procurement or staffing process, government managers must think long and hard about the "make or buy" decision – whether it is most advantageous to develop capacity or products internally to support long-term delivery, or whether a suitable product or service exists in the marketplace that could bring greater benefits to the department than efforts undertaken within.

In some cases, individual projects require access to specialized areas of expertise that are not available through resources already in-house and for which a staff position does not exist, necessitating access to external contractors to fill the requirement. This may be in support of short-term initiatives, such as a study or assessment, or a concrete piece of development work to enable ongoing delivery or maintenance of a solution by the buying organization. Other operational requirements may be longer term, requiring the deployment of significant levels of resources not available internally; in these situations, a decision may be made to outsource an entire operation with the government organization responsible for the delivery of a service to Canadians, through a contractor.

Like many private sector industries, government departments are also feeling the squeeze from reduced numbers of internal resources due to the demographic shift in the composition of public service membership and increasing numbers of retirements among "Baby Boomers" and "Busters." Coupled with smaller staffing budgets, contracting out for the services of experienced and qualified resources under temporary help or other competitive services contracting arrangements has become a common, practical, and valid means for filling short-term needs while allowing the time for longer-term solutions to be implemented.

Due to the nature of the work, independent contractors may work in collaboration with and sometimes alongside public service employees to achieve shared objectives and outcomes. Contractors may even, in some cases, be doing ostensibly the same type of work as individuals who operate under a very different type of contract. As George's story shows, however, when the line between the buyer and the seller becomes blurred and the contractor-client arrangement takes on the form of an employer-employee relationship, difficulties can arise for both parties.

A procurement contract is defined as a "contract for service" or business arrangement, whether short or long term, entered into to complete specific work in exchange for payment. In contrast, an employment contract is a "contract of service" – a relationship, whether short or long term, entered into to complete specific work in return for payment. Both are governed by the same principles of contract law (Ontario Ministry of Revenue, 2000; Human Resources and Social Development Canada, 2006). And in those two small words perhaps lies the potential for the confusion and the risk that one may become the other, whether it was originally intended that way or not. Procurement contracts for services may need to be entered into for a variety of reasons. This in and of itself is not a bad thing; in fact, in the right circumstances it can be quite beneficial to all parties (buyer, seller, and the Canadian taxpayer) when contracting is aimed at achieving best value (Treasury Board Secretariat, 2003a, s. 16.1.5).

However, *Contracting Policy* (s. 4.1.9) requires buying organizations to "ensure that an employer-employee relationship will not result when contracting for the services of individuals in accordance with criteria established by the Canada Customs and Revenue Agency and pertinent court rulings" (Treasury Board Secretariat, 2003b). Under the policy, the accountability to ensure this will not and does not occur rests with the Contracting Authority, or the individual within the buying organization whose role it is to establish and administer the contract. One would think, then, that mitigating the risk of the formation of employer-employee relationships would be no more than ensuring that the right clauses and conditions are included in the contract.

It is not only what is on paper, however, that determines the status of a relationship and the accountabilities of each party to it, but also how the paper relationship is managed in practice.

The responsibility for establishing and managing contracts in many federal buying organizations is often divided between the Contracting Authority and the Project or Technical Authority who needs the work to be completed. This division of responsibilities may be true both of contracts for discrete projects and in the case of anticipatory contracting mechanisms such as Standing Offer Agreements (SOAs) or Supply Arrangements (SAs), where in many departments and agencies the mechanism is "owned" and call-ups are issued by a central Contracting Authority, but day-to-day interaction with the contractor is handled by the Project or Technical Authority.

While the Contracting Authority develops the contract terms and conditions, runs any competition, and establishes and manages the contractual aspects of the agreement with an external contractor, it is often the latter Authority who develops the Statement of Work for the contract, acts as the day-to-day contact with the contractor for the work being undertaken, and who may review and accept the contractor's deliverables and services. In some cases these individuals may even be located within separate branches of the organization, or in a different region of the country. Both roles of interacting with a contractor can pose a risk of forming an employer-employee relationship. While these management arrangements can be practical and highly effective from an operational viewpoint, where the ultimate accountability lies with the Contracting Authority to mitigate the formation of these risky relationships, the division of contract management can mean that by the time the accountable party becomes aware of any potential and unintended employment issue within a procurement contract, it may already be too late.

This risk appears relatively reduced in procurement contracts for the acquisition of goods or construction purchased to support government activities. These contract relationships appear fairly well defined, with a relatively low risk of negative financial or legal consequences to the buyer if the product or work is delivered. In most cases under these types of procurement contracts, the contractor delivers the high-tech system or builds the bridge; the work is inspected by the buyer; the work is accepted (or corrections required, and made by the contractor prior to acceptance); the contractor is paid and moves on to the next order or job. The greatest potential for longer term or day-to-day interaction with contractors to undertake the necessary planning, updates, review and approval activities – and thus a greater risk for an employer-employee relationship to form unknowingly – appears, then, to be in the acquisition of services.

Despite neither party to the contractor-client relationship intending for it to transform into an employer-employee relationship, it is a risk, and is perceived to be a significant one, when government (or any) buyers establish contracts for services. The perception of risk is heightened when contracting for the services of individuals (versus teams of contractors or entire companies). The alarm bells start ringing more urgently when contracting for professional services, typically requiring the services of specific specialized individuals, and even more so when establishing contracts for the services of a former public servant – someone who has made the switch from being an employee to being an independent contractor.

There are several well-used tests established by courts and tribunals to determine the status of contractual relationships. The difference between an employee and an independent contractor may be summed up in the following four principles. Each of these principles should be examined individually, but together they combine for a full assessment of whether an existing relationship is better defined as employer-employee or contractor-client:

- *Control over the work* – Who determines not only what has to be done, but also how?
- *Equipment and tools* – Who provides, maintains, and retains them?
- *Integration* – Is the work integral to the organization's overall service delivery responsibility, or is the person providing the work integral to the organization's processes and environment?
- *Financial independence* – Who benefits from and who carries the financial risk? (Canada Revenue Agency, 2006; HRSDC, 2006; Ontario Ministry of Revenue, 2000)

Depending upon the specific context of the contract and the relationship, when one, some, or all of the above may be answered by "the buyer," chances are the procurement contract has already become an employment contract. But it might not have to be this way. If there is an awareness among both parties about the potential for this change in status to occur, and a means to distinguish one from the other once it has already happened, there must be something that can be done to minimize or mitigate the risk of an employment relationship forming under what began as a procurement contract, before it is signed and while the ink is still fresh.

Start Off on the Right Foot

The following practices are suggested to help reduce the risk of an employer-employee relationship forming under a procurement contract, by addressing one or more of the four above principles that help define these relationships.

1. State the intent of the contractual relationship up front. Canada Revenue Agency (2006) notes that the usual first step in determining the status of parties within a contractual relationship is to examine the intent of the parties when it was established. This includes an assessment as to whether the intent of the contractual arrangement was clearly known to both parties, and whether it was held in common. One means to support this clear and common understanding is to ensure it forms an integral part of the contract documents themselves. Most government contracts include some variation on a standard clause, which identifies that the contractor is not an employee of the government and that the contractor is responsible for deductions and remittances (Public Works and Government Services Canada, 2006).

Including the resulting contract terms and conditions as part of any competitive Request for Proposals can highlight this (and other) intentions of the buying organization with respect to the resulting relationship, and provides for transparency of contract terms in the competitive procurement process. In submitting a proposal, the resulting contractor is identifying that he or she has read and understands the terms of the contract – a common understanding.

2. Establish fixed-price contracts, where possible. As noted above, one of the defining characteristics of the status of a contractor-client relationship is the existence of both the opportunity for profit and the risk of loss on the part of the contractor (Canada Revenue Agency, 2006; Ontario Ministry of Revenue, 2000). In an employment relationship, individuals are sheltered to a much greater degree from the vagaries of the marketplace than is an independent consultant. For an employee, if business is good, the employee receives his or her salary and benefits. If business is less favourable the next year, notwithstanding a grave economic crisis, the employee should receive the same salary and benefits as stipulated in the employment agreement between the employer and the individual. Contractors, however, are more exposed to the whims of the marketplace, and in engaging in their work, to the opportunity for profit. This is one key component of performance-based contracting – in submitting a proposal or undertaking the work, the contractor promises the ability to deliver outcomes and end products or services that will meet the client's objectives, as established in the contract. To support achieving this outcome and simultaneously mitigating the risk of an employer-employee relationship forming, a fixed price should be established for the work. In contrast to a per diem or time-based basis of payment, which could be viewed as establishing a salary payable for ongoing work more suited to an employment relationship, a fixed price is payable only upon the delivery of a specific piece of the work.

Under this basis of payment, the government buyer may have more assurance that the costs associated with the completion of the specified deliverables will not be subject to any future escalation. This basis of payment also places maximum accountability on the contractor to control the cost of the work, and thus how the work is to be done (Office of the Auditor General of Canada, 1996; Public Works and Government Services Canada, 2006).

While a fixed price may be seen as the best means to set up the contract basis of payment to mitigate the risk of an employment relationship, it may not always be possible. For example, in multiphased projects where the scope and timing of subsequent phases may depend on the outcomes of the first phase, a fixed price may not be realistic or could actually serve to inflate costs when it is established in order to cover future unknowns; or where contracts are placed to provide day-to-day operational-type services over the short term, specific deliverables may not be defined in the contract.

Contracts based on time rates are therefore entirely appropriate for specific types of services; they just require a different type of management by the buyer to achieve results and maintain the contractor-client relationship status.

3. Establish a sound Statement of Work, and let both parties work to it. In best practice, a Statement of Work defines the scope of a contractor's engagement and what the outputs or outcomes will be, but remains relatively silent on how the work is to be conducted. This silence on the part of the buyer is intended to be filled by the Contractor's Proposal, which should detail the methods that will be undertaken to achieve the outcomes and provide the deliverables required, and by the work of the contractor once the contract is in place. While some requirements may need a greater degree of specificity by the buyer in relation to "how," such as the use of specific recognized methodologies, techniques or tools (for example, to ensure congruency to departmental standards or other components of related work under a project), buyers should refrain from overspecifying approaches, methodologies, and tools to be used, as there should still be something unique, specialized, or innovative the contractor is bringing to the table in terms of how the work will be conducted that provides for value under the contract.

This approach and methodology can also be a critical aspect of what differentiates one supplier from another in a competitive procurement process and can provide for an effective evaluation criterion to select the contractor that provides best value. A complementary approach within the Statement of Work might also be to include a formal Service-Level Agreement (SLA), which can, if appropriate to the work, also be tied to financial holdbacks or incentives. Under such an SLA, the contractor retains ultimate accountability for results and maintains the potential for risk of profit or loss, as he or she may have to forego the profit on the contract in full if the outcome is not delivered.

While a limited Statement of Work and a Service-Level Agreement may be best targeted for discrete contracts or one-off projects to which a contractor can propose a solution, this does not necessarily mean that less defined contracts need be unscoped. For anticipatory contracting mechanisms, such as SOAs or SAs, which are typically established with time rates, each Call-up or Task forms a separate contract. Where possible, the Project Authority should meet with the contractor at the outset of each Call-up or Task to fully scope out the work and enable him or her to provide a Proposal, including approach and (potentially fixed) price.

If the work is already under way in the absence of such a defined framework, one possible method of enhancing the contractor's accountability for results is to request, as a paid deliverable, the development of a work plan, to be developed by the contractor, that lays out the specific deliverables or milestones the buyer can expect to receive as the work progresses. Outcomes achieved can then be measured against the work plan, helping the Project Authority (the buyer) to maintain his/her right to exercise control over the end result of the product/service, and the contractor to maintain control over how the work is completed.

4. Watch whose pen is used, but not too closely. The buyer sometimes needs to provide resources, specialized tools, or equipment to enable the contractor to complete his or her work. While our story's protagonist used relatively simple tools, reflective of the type of services he was providing, in some cases buyers might need to provide access to specialized software, systems, raw materials for manufacturing or testing, background materials, or even documentation that is being developed under a contract.

On the contractor's side, much work has been completed by government, which could contribute valuable background to support current undertakings. Resources such as previous studies, reports, and other materials can not only support the planning and conduct of contracted work to meet the established contract objectives, but in some cases essential components of the work may have already been completed, whether internally or under previous contracts. Where it is possible to share these earlier results and developments with the contractor, it can reduce or mitigate the potential for rework, and support the achievement of the primary objective of contracting – best value to the Crown and the Canadian people (Treasury Board Secretariat, 2003b, s. 1).

Where possible, the buyer should document any available and needed resources in advance within the Statement of Work – both the tools and resources the government can commit to providing, and those that the contractor will be required to supply. Where contracts are already under way, managers can work with the contractor at the planning and scoping stages of projects or service delivery, and at milestones in the work, to identify what resources are required that may already be in existence. In most contracts, the primary location of work should be the contractor's own premises; however, in some cases there are valid operational or security requirements necessitating the buying organization to provide the space in which the work will take place. When contracted resources need to work on site to access needed resources or to support a day-to-day operational function, the buyer should avoid "hands-on" oversight and direction, which can lead unintentionally to a transfer of control over how the work is done. Instead, formal review of deliverables should take place at identified milestones in the contract or the project. Hands-off management applies equally to the contractor – the buyer should not ask the contractor to supervise the work of organizational employees.

As noted above, although ownership and maintenance of tools can be a factor in determining whether an employment relationship exists, it is not the only factor (Ontario Ministry of Revenue, 2000). But the point is, if it drives like an employee, it might be one.

In a similar vein, contractors should provide their own business cards and, where required and where possible, their own phone access, and not be listed in an organization's directory unless they are clearly identified as contractors.

If a contractor is working on site or when attending meetings, it is reasonable for the buyer to greet the contractor politely and even warmly, and treat him or her with the same respect as one would an employee.

While George's unfortunate story ended up with a supportive outcome for George and his family, if not for the manager left answering pointed questions from his ministry, being dubbed an "employee" is most often neither intended nor desired by either party in what was originally established as a contractor-client relationship. Investigations into the status of working relationships can be initiated by the buyer (government) or the seller (contractor) or may come about through random audit activities. While government managers are largely aware of the impacts of such a ruling on their departments' budgets, it is important to note that the impact on the contractor's side is not necessarily positive. Being "turned" suddenly into an employee can result in unforeseen tax complications for the contractor and may also lead to great difficulty in establishing future contracts for his or her business.

The risk of transition of a contractor-client relationship to employer-employee status has true concerns for both parties, which need to be respected. However, all of this is not to say that cordial and professional business relationships cannot be established with contractors. Sound management, as applied to every project, program, and service, can be equally applied to the contracts through which they are delivered. When both parties to the procurement contract relationship have a common understanding, intent, and interest in maintaining its status, the risk of forming an employer-employee relationship can be, if not eliminated, mitigated.

For more information on mitigating the risk of employer-employee relationships during the development or at the outset of your contracting arrangements, speak with your Contracting Authority and review your contract's Statement of Work looking for enforceability and management of performance-work processes. Should you have any concerns regarding the status of one of your organization's current relationships with a contracted party, contact your internal Human Resources representative, Human Resources and Social Development Canada, or your organization's legal services for a context-based analysis.

References

Canada Revenue Agency. 2006. "Employee or Self-Employed." Publication No. RC4110(E), rev. December 2006. Accessed at http://www.craarc.gc.ca/E/pub/tg/rc4110/.

Human Resources and Social Development Canada (HRSDC). April 2006. "Determining the Employer/Employee Relationship – Canada Labour Code." Accessed at http://www.hrsdc.gc.ca/en/lp/lo/opdipg/ipg/069.shtml.

Ministry of Revenue, Ontario. 2000. "How to Identify an Employer-Employee Relationship." Accessed at http://www.rev.gov.on.ca/english/bulletins/eht/0196.htm.

Office of the Auditor General of Canada. 1996. "Systems under Development: Getting Results." In *1996 November Report of the Office of the Auditor General of Canada*, Chapter 26.

Public Works and Government Services Canada. 2006. "Preparing the Contract." In *New Buyers Guide,* Chapter 12. Accessed at http://www.contractscanada.gc.ca/en/chap12-e.htm.

Treasury Board Secretariat. 2003a. "Changes Required to be Current with Legislation, Policies and Changing Marketplace Conditions." *Contracting Policy Notice 2003-3*, June 4. Accessed at http:www.tbssct.gc.ca/pubs_pol/dcgpubs/ContPol.

— 2003b. *Contracting Policy*, June 9. Accessed at http://www.tbssct.gc.ca/pol/doc-eng.aspx?id=12027.

Case Sampler #11

An International Lessons-Learned Case

DREAMING BIG, IMPLEMENTING NOT-SO-BIG: DEVELOPMENT COORDINATION IN JORDAN'S MINISTRY OF LABOUR

by Leslie Shimotakahara

Introduction

Canada is playing a leading role in assisting with Jordan's Employment – Technical and Vocational Education and Training strategy (E-TVET). Developed over the past few years under the umbrella of the National Agenda, this progressive and ambitious reform strategy aims to increase Jordan's competitiveness by creating a knowledge-based economy that matches the labour market demands of the twenty-first century. Since Jordan presently has one of the lowest labour market participation rates in the region (40 percent), and an increasingly youthful population (nearly 38 percent of the population is younger than age 15), E-TVET is all the more crucial to the future of Jordan.

While E-TVET was developed by a variety of stakeholders, the Ministry of Labour was put in charge of leading the reform. To fulfill its leadership role, the Ministry needed to enhance its administrative and management capacities writ large; the first step was to set up a Development Coordination Unit to oversee and coordinate all activities. Thus, as a part of its longstanding commitment to Jordan, the Canadian International Development Agency (CIDA) decided to sponsor an Advisor to the Ministry of Labour through the Deployment for Democratic Development (DDD), CIDA's flagship rapid-response

---

This case is part of the case study series Deployment for Democratic Development, a program of the International Division of IPAC. Leslie Shimotakahara was a Program Officer in the International Programs division of the Institute of Public Administration of Canada when she wrote this case in 2009.

program, jointly administered by the Institute of Public Administration of Canada and Rights & Democracy. Canadian expert Brenda Cooke was deployed to provide technical support to the local executive director of the Development Coordination Unit in setting up and operationalizing the unit. This involved developing a Reform Program Implementation Model, including an organizational design for the unit, and providing *inter alia* policy guidance, advice on financial management and reporting arrangements, and on-the-fly training on a host of human resource management issues. Having previously worked in Jordan, India, Yemen, and Sri Lanka on educational reform projects, following an impressive career as a public servant and the president of two colleges in Canada, Ms. Cooke brought more than 30 years of international and Canadian experience to this initiative. She resided in Jordan as the Ministry of Labour's in-house consultant from May to August 2008.

PROJECT PROFILE

Title: Supporting the Establishment and Operationalization of a Development Coordination Unit at Jordan's Ministry of Labour

Client: H.E. Mr. Majed Habashneh, Secretary General, Ministry of Labour

Consultant: Brenda Cooke, Education Consultant

Duration: March–August 2008

Budget: $ 74,369.58

Key Outputs: The existing Terms of Reference and Mandate of the DCU reviewed, revised, and approved by stakeholders.

An Implementation Model for the Reform Program developed.

A set of job descriptions developed for all positions in the DCU.

All key positions filled according to established hiring processes.

Existing staff on the Initiative assigned clear roles within the DCU where appropriate.

At the end of the project, Ms. Cooke reported highly positive results – 80 percent of planned objectives had been achieved. These successful results are all the more remarkable in light of the bumps that the project encountered along the way, as Ms. Cooke explained in her final report and elaborated during an interview.

Soon after her arrival, it became clear that Ministry of Labour stakeholders were expecting to implement a project of much grander scale and ten times the budget. Envisioned as a Sector-Wide Approach (SWAp), E-TVET was initially conceived as a strategy through which development agencies across the board would collaborate to support sector-wide reform among all the stakeholder groups based on Jordan's long-term vision for its development in the employment, technical and vocational education and training sector.

While taking such a holistic and harmonized approach is no doubt commendable in theory, SWAps can be challenging to implement. But through Ms. Cooke's provision of a modest amount of technical assistance under DDD, the project was salvaged – yielding some valuable lessons learned.

Managing Stakeholders' Expectations

How much should E-TVET try to accomplish? And how broadly do development partners wish to spread their assistance? When Ms. Cooke arrived on the scene in Jordan, one of her biggest challenges was to deal with the overly ambitious expectations that had been built up among stakeholders. Over the previous two years, during its planning and inception phase, the E-TVET reform had inspired all stakeholder groups to "dream big" and identify activities in which they could participate. A plethora of stakeholders including the colleges, the Vocational Training Corporation, the school system vocational program, unions, and chambers were encouraged to identify ways they could be part of the reform plan. Concurrently, a host of development partners – CIDA, the World Bank, the European Union, Japan International Cooperation Agency, and United States Agency for International Development among others – were identifying areas that would contribute to E-TVET's success in which they wished to become involved. In the end, the SWAp envisioned was costed at US$163 million.

As the project moved toward implementation, however, it became evident that the available funds were significantly more modest. At project start-up, the project had two main development partners – CIDA and the World Bank – who were able to contribute jointly US$16 million. The European Union, which played a leading role in the original plan-building, is expecting to contribute to E-TVET about 35 million euros starting late in 2009 through a budget-support mechanism which will give a lump sum of money to the Ministry of Labour to allocate according to Ministry priorities.

As Ms. Cooke reflects, "It was difficult to take over from the previous two-year process of developing broad project plans and stakeholder buy-in. In moving from the 'visioning' stage to the 'implementation' stage, the scope of the project had to be scaled down to a realistic size, commensurate with the development partners' committed funds." At the same time, it was challenging to "maintain the momentum and commitment of all stakeholder groups" who had been allowed to dream in colour. Developing the work plan took time and patience because there was a myriad of competing models that various development partners had already developed and championed. Despite such complexities, SWAps remain an appealing route for development partners looking to support projects with far-reaching objectives and potential benefits. In best case scenarios, according to one World Bank paper, SWAps "strengthen government ownership and coordination of projects, facilitate budgeting of sufficient funds to cover operating costs, integrate capital investment budgets in overall country budgets, and support policies and efforts to build domestic capacity."[1]

Popular among World Bank projects since the mid 1990s, SWAps include such success stories as Bangladesh Health, Ghana Health, Pakistan Social Action, Ethiopia Education, Zambia Agriculture, Mozambique Agriculture, and Tanzania Health. But the flipside of such sector-wide programming is that the "cost and time taken to prepare these operations, and their supervision costs, are significantly above the average for the rest of the portfolio."[2]

The challenges of implementing E-TVET were compounded because it was anything but a typical SWAp. The ideal SWAp is organized by a clear sequence of events: first, development partners come forward with funds; second, priorities and a holistic project plan are developed by the country; and finally, the development community plays a supportive role in helping to oversee and coordinate the system-wide reform. But in the case of E-TVET, planning began from the bottom up: various stakeholders identified activities they wished to champion, fuelled by the commitment of one or two prominent development partners. The result was a plan whose scope far outstretched what could be realistically implemented within the funds available. Thus whenever creating a sector reform strategy, regardless of whether it is stakeholder or donor-driven, Ms. Cooke cautions, it is probably good advice to "avoid being too ambitious." Her advice is substantiated by a working paper on SWAps by the Danish International Development Agency, in which the authors warn against being "too elaborate at the outset," emphasizing that the "essential components" of sound sector-wide programming are a "statement of sector policy that all partners can support, and an agreed co-ordination and dialogue framework through which the sector development programme can be developed and subsequently managed."[3] Fairly early on in the process, it is advisable that a "comprehensive, costed and prioritized programme" be established to "discipline government and donors alike," as an evolving guideline for the partnership.[4]

Once the plan is created, whether by stakeholders or development partners, it is crucial to cost it out, revise accordingly, and produce a final plan of realistic scope to which development partners are willing to commit. Although E-TVET followed a more haphazard route in terms of funding, it had a solid statement of sector policy that proved instrumental in helping Ms. Cooke to keep the project on track. CIDA is also to credited, she notes, for making a "contribution to the project in a way that has sufficient flexibility to meet unexpected needs and to fill gaps as they are identified."

Implementing a Change in Approach

Ms. Cooke took a highly participatory approach to setting up and operationalizing the Development Coordination Unit. Since the unit was to be housed right within the Ministry of Labour, her task was to work with Ministry employees on a day-to-day basis and bring them on board through the development of administrative and staffing procedures, as well as individual and institutional work plans and an operation manual. In order for all this to go smoothly, it had to become apparent to the Ministry staff that the scale down of E-TVET was necessary, rather than appearing to be imposed from the outside.

Explaining the change in terms of a transition from "visioning" to "implementation" helped to make people comfortable with the scaled-down approach. By "respecting and finding a place for the previous work," Ms. Cooke managed to keep "the focus away from the personal and on the task at hand." It helped to get people involved in the real and practical work of implementing the project – developing procurement plans and writing terms of reference for consultancies, for instance. On a day-to-day basis and while running workshops, she was guided by "metacognitive approaches to implementing change, which involves naming, describing, and explaining change and discussing people's reaction" in order to create an accepting and inclusive environment. The Stakeholders' Workshop in Aqaba was a turning point in this respect. The workshop was highly participatory, with stakeholders able to work within and across stakeholder groups to identify problems and priorities, which were taken forward to the E-TVET Council for consideration.

The Development Coordination Unit is now fully operational: all positions have been successfully staffed and Mr. Ghazi Daboubi, a seasoned human resource professional formerly at the Central Bank of Jordan, has been hired as executive director. The reform program is up and running, and exercises in capacity building are underway. An implementation plan for the project has been developed, and three large-scale interventions have been identified and are currently out to tender.

At the conclusion of Ms. Cooke's assignment for Deployment for Democratic Development, the Minister of Labour asked CIDA to supply a co-operant to stay on for two more years, providing ongoing advice and support to the Ministry and the Development Coordination Unit in the implementation of the project. Commending Jordan's "high regard for Canadian expertise in the E-TVET field," Ms. Cooke applied for and was selected for the assignment. One of her first tasks was to draft terms of reference for a large assignment within the E-TVET plan – the restructuring of the Vocational Training Corporation (VTC), which owns and manages 45 training centres/institutes that are not at present being efficiently utilized. This contract allowed her to make use of lessons learned from her recent assignment and to move the project from plan to implementation.

At the recommendation of the Minister of Labour, Ms. Cooke developed the terms of reference for the VTC restructuring assignment using a "design/implement" approach. What is envisioned is a team of long-term technical experts working as "the support team" alongside designated incumbents – "the counterpart team" – who are responsible for the key areas of reform: governance, organizational development, finance, human resources, management, training, and industry liaison. The support team will work collaboratively with the counterpart team to create a new employer-driven business model, governance model, and training service delivery model based on a modular approach that includes laddered sets of competencies with various exit points and levels of certification. This project is more likely to remain on a realistic scale, since its pieces will be implemented as funding is identified. By twinning technical experts with their local counterparts, the methodology aims to produce a reform tailored to local expectations and needs.

Reflecting on her final thoughts about E-TVET, Ms. Cooke says, "It's a fine line to walk between developing a plan that the stakeholders want and one that the development partners want to fund." The task is to work with both groups in tandem to ensure that grand plans aren't developed upon the needs identified by stakeholders alone, irrespective of development partner backing.

By the time Ms. Cooke departed Jordan, the E-TVET project environment had been significantly improved. It is impressive that so much could be accomplished through DDD's provision of a skilled advisor for a relatively short-term assignment, which is precisely the niche that DDD was designed to fulfill. This initiative can be seen as a true success story about what a modicum of the right assistance at the right time can accomplish. By assisting the local partner to identify and surmount obstacles that had arisen in the course of their own development goals, Ms. Cooke provided just the infusion of technical support required to move from plan to implementation.

Lessons Learned

- Tight deadlines can be productive in moving from plan to implementation. When you've had a long planning period (in fact, too long), it's not a bad idea to have a relatively short period to move to implementation. It gets people focused fast.
- Keep your eye on the bottom line. Once you know exactly what the resource level of the project is going to be, at least at start-up, you have to narrow down your project scope to match.
- But don't lose sight of the big plan. You have to keep the big plan in mind so that it can be activated once other development partners come on board – and you need a forum for that discussion to happen.
- Take an inclusive approach to dealing with change. When project plans need to be modified or scaled down, take the time to discuss employees' and stakeholders' responses to the changes and why they are necessary. Find ways to settle and obtain recognition of work already done.

Notes

[1] "Fiduciary Arrangements for Sector-Wide Approaches (SWAps)" (World Bank, Operations Policy and Country Services, April 2002), 2.

[2] Ibid, 4.

[3] "The Sector-Wide Approach: Organizing Principle for Bilateral Development Cooperation" (DANIDA, Sector-wide Approach Support Group, 2004), 24.

[4] Ibid., 25.

Appendix

Inventory of Public Administration Case Study Sites

APPENDIX
Inventory of Public Administration Case Study Sites

Title of Site	Address	Subject Areas	Relevance to Public Administration	No. of Cases	Potential Use of Cases	General Utility of Site
American Society for Public Administration (ASPA) Center for Accountability and Performance	www.aspanet.org	Ethics and accountability	All cases are focused on public administration (see the Publications section of the website). Cases examine ethics within the field of public administration	17	Training/research	Designed for use by professionals in the public sector Note: ASPA membership required
Case Method Website: How to Teach with Cases, University of California, Santa Barbara	http://www.soc.ucsb.edu/projects/casemethod/	Trade, immigration, human rights, international cases	Public affairs, policy management, public administration	20+	Research/education	Researchers, educators Free access
Case Method of Instruction (CMI) Outreach Project, Vanderbilt University	http://www.cmiproject.net/instructor_materials.htm	Training, leadership, situational analysis	Policy, working in a public administration environment	20+	For instruction purposes only	For educators Free
Case Net	http://casenet.thomsonlearning.com/	Accounting, business, law ethics, management, marketing/business, humanities, social sciences, technology	Political science, public policy, public administration	20+	Instruction/research	Students, educators Fees charged
Case Studies in Public Policy Development by Ginsler & Associates Inc	http://www.ginsler.com/html/partv_a.htp	Social policy	Public administration	20+	Public servants, students, researchers	This consulting company has many case studies on its website, but many of these studies do not work.

Title of Site	Address	Subject Areas	Relevance to Public Administration	No. of Cases	Potential Use of Cases	General Utility of Site
Case Studies in Science, State University of New York – Buffalo	http://library.buffalo.edu/libraries/projects/cases/case.html	Case method in teaching	Case studies for teaching science		Teaching	Provides access to training materials
Center for Technology in Government	http://www.ctg.albany.edu/publications/publications?sub=cases	Technology	Use of IT in government	20+	Research	Provides research material
Colorado Department of Natural Resources	http://dnrgoogle.state.co.us/search?q=Case%20studies&site=my_collection&client=my_collection&proxystylesheet=http://dnr.state.co.us/Styles/dnr.xslt&output=xml_no_dtd&restrict=dnr	Wildlife preservation policy/environmental policy	Environmental focus	20+	Research	Discusses the activities of the Colorado Department of Natural Resources
Connecticut Department of Environment Protection	http://www.ct.gov/dep/search/search.asp?qu=case+studies&go.x=0&go.y=0	Water management, pollution prevention	Water policy	10+	Research	Government website studies, and the department of Natural Resources
Delaware Department of Natural Resources and Environmental Protection	http://search.delaware.gov/search?as_sitesearch=http%3A%2F%2Fwww.dnrec.delaware.gov&q=caes+studies&srch_btn.x=0&srch_btn.y=0	Natural resource management	Resource management by public institutions	1	Research	State-based website
Dispute Resolution Program, Canada	http://www.lfcc.on.ca/children_exposed_to_domestic_violence.html	Case studies with regard to children and domestic abuse	Social policy on dealing with abused children	20+	Research	Free

Title of Site	Address	Subject Areas	Relevance to Public Administration	No. of Cases	Potential Use of Cases	General Utility of Site
Electronic Hallway	http://www.hallway.org	Numerous policy areas: economic development, education, environment and land use, human services, international affairs, nonprofit, state and local government issues, utility and transit issues, and urban and regional issues	Various policy areas, many with a public administration theme	500+	Mostly educational	Teaching aids Annual fee
European Case Clearing House	http://www.ecch.com/about/case-search-logging-in.cfm#%23	Similar to the database at the Kennedy school	Policy, politics, public administration	Largest in world – over 26,000	Research	Required login, and cases are for purchase
Florida Office of Program Policy Analysis and Government Accountability (OPPAGA)	http://www.oppaga.state.fl.us/TopicList.aspx	Performance of state agencies and programs	Various project-based case studies conducted by OPPAGA, a research unit of the Florida legislature	+20	Research	Focuses on identifying ways to improve services and cut costs
Governmental Accounting Standards Boards	http://www.seagov.org/sea_gasb_project/other_studies.shtml	Performance measurement for government services	Risk management in the public sector	+20	Research/course pack info	Publication of performance-related case studies; numerous links to case studies funded by the Alfred P. Sloan Foundation Free

Title of Site	Address	Subject Areas	Relevance to Public Administration	No. of Cases	Potential Use of Cases	General Utility of Site
Hazardous Site Health Evaluation Program, New Jersey	http://www.nj.gov/health/eoh/hhazweb/hlthstud.htm	Health policy in New Jersey	Epidemiology	10	Research	Government research
Institute for the Study of Diplomacy, Georgetown University	http://www.guisd.org/index.cfm?action=Shop&thisPage=SubCat&MenuCategory=2&MenuCategoryName='Case%20Studies'	Trade and international relations	Policy	50+	Research	Login, and cases for purchase
International Consortium of Governmental Financial Management	http://www.icgfm.org/reports.htm	Government finance	Financial policy Note: This database does not necessarily have case studies but publications and presentations on the topic of government finance. There is some discussion of case studies in the presentation notes.		Research	Corporate education, public servants in finance
International Records Management Trusts	http://www.irmt.org/educationTrainMaterials.html	Ethics/management practices	Management of public institutions	29	Training	Training materials for management practices
Journalism.org	http://www.journalism.org/research_and_analysis/Studies	Public institutions in the media	Media relations	30+	Research/ training	Publication of qualitative studies and research
Learning and Teaching Support Network Centre for Economics	http://www.economics-network.ac.uk/handbook/casestudies/	Economics	Economics	20+	Training, useful to professors of economics	Teaching materials
Louisiana Department of Environmental Quality	http://www.hydrolab.com/case_studies/default.asp	Water policy	Cases discuss water management and the usage of water resources	13	Project descriptions	Descriptions of projects, with cases and analysis

Title of Site	Address	Subject Areas	Relevance to Public Administration	No. of Cases	Potential Use of Cases	General Utility of Site
Minnesota Department of Natural Resources	http://www.pca.state.mn.us/oea/berc/transpac.cfm	Transportation policy	Transportation-related case study with a focus on cost cutting: preventing waste and pollution makes more than economic sense – recycling and environmental purchasing can boost employee morale, improve worker safety, and reduce liability	1	Research	Case study of a particular policy
Minnesota Department of Transportation	http://www.planning.dot.gov/Documents/Rural/MNDOT.htm	A report on public involvement in Minnesota		1	Research	Case descriptions
National Academy of Public Administration	http://www.napawash.org/pc_economy_environment/learning_texts.html	Diverse policy areas, including innovation, trade, the environment	Contains significant publications related to areas of public administration	20+	Research	For purchase
National Aeronautics and Space Administration: Goddard Library	http://library.gsfc.nasa.gov/public/cspub.htm	Project management, organizational culture		10	Knowledge management	Free
National Alliance to End Homelessness, Canada	http://www.endhomelessness ottawa.ca/index.cfm	Policies regarding the homeless	Use of public institutions to deal with homelessness	2	Research	Promotes the work of the Alliance
National Center for Public Productivity	http://andromeda.rutgers.edu/~ncpp/cdgp/cases.html	Citizen engagement	Involving people in the policy-making process	15+	Research/training	Publication of case studies

Title of Site	Address	Subject Areas	Relevance to Public Administration	No. of Cases	Potential Use of Cases	General Utility of Site
The National Civic League	http://www.ncl.org/npp/publications.html	Politics/civic engagement	Politicians' relationships with public administrators	5	Research	Sale of this institution's publications – deliberative democratic community institute
The National Council for Public-Private Partnerships (PPP)	http://www.ncppp.org/cases/index.shtml	PPPs in public works, safety, water, transportation infrastructure, operation management	PPPs as a field of public administration	20+	Research	Promotes PPP
National Endowment for the Arts	http://www.nea.gov/research/researchreports_chrono.html	Administration of arts-based institutions	Administration of the arts as a publically funded institution	+20	Research/course materials	Promotion of the arts in the US Free
National Governors Association (NGA) Center for Best Practices	http://www.nga.org/portal/site/nga/menuitem.6398ca27f6d963268a278110501010a0/?vgnextoid=e0dcaf4def7d0010VgnVCM1000001a01010aRCRD&vgnextfmt=publications	Public policy administration and management	Assorted cases, with a focus on policy	+25	Research	Case studies are scattered throughout the site and may be difficult to locate
Nelson A. Rockefeller Institute of Government	http://rockinst.org/researchanddata/	State and local government finance, federalism, intergovernmental relations	Public administration–related research	+20	Research	Focuses on New York State (e.g., statistics, health care education, disaster recovery, faith-based social services, workforce welfare and social services, cities and neighbourhoods)

Title of Site	Address	Subject Areas	Relevance to Public Administration	No. of Cases	Potential Use of Cases	General Utility of Site
New York City Office of Emergency Management	http://search1.nyc.gov/search?output=xml_no_dtd&site=default_collection&proxystylesheet=agency_frontend&client=agency_frontend&sitesearch=home2.nyc.gov%2Fhtml%2Foem&q=%22case+studies%22	Risk management	Emergency management	2	Policy/public administration, gov. research guideline	Government database
NOAA Coastal Service Center, South Carolina	http://www.csc.noaa.gov/products/nchaz/htm/case.htm	Environmental risk management	A case study vulnerability assessment, with GIS project file and data	1	Research tool	Government database with links to other data and case studies
Pew Center for Civic Journalism	http://www.pewcenter.org/doingcj/pubs/cases/intro.html	Journalism/public administration	Civic engagement	6	Research	Site sells publications and promotes the organization as a think tank
Sustainable Communities Network	http://www.sustainable.org/casestudies/studiesindex.html	Community-based case studies dealing with various policy issues and resource management	Public policy issues	50+	Research/training	
Transparency International	http://www.transparency.org/publications/publications	Topics of corruption and poor accountability/responsibility	Public administration, ethics	20+	Research	Publishes the institutes' publications
United Nations Educational Scientific and Cultural Organization	http://portal.unesco.org/education/en/ev.php-URL_ID=12085&URL_DO=DO_TOPIC&URL_SECTION=201.html	UN cases in the area of educational programs	Educational policy development	5	Research	UN publications

Title of Site	Address	Subject Areas	Relevance to Public Administration	No. of Cases	Potential Use of Cases	General Utility of Site
United Nations Public Administration Program (UNPAN) Case Studies	http://www.unpan.org/dpepa_worldpareport.asp	Globalization, e-government, civic engagement, public governance, public sector performance	Public administration	4	Research/course materials	Research/course materials
The Urban Institute	http://search.urban.org/texis/search?mode=&opts=&pr=wwwurban&dropXSL=html&prox=page&rorder=500&rprox=500&rdfreq=500&rwfreq=750&rlead=750&sufs=0&order=r&query=%22case+studies%22+&submit=Submit	Urban issues	Various public policy concerns in an urban environment: crime, poverty, etc.	Many	Research	Promotes the work of affiliated authors. Research oriented
US Federal Emergency Management Agency	http://www.fema.gov/plan/prevent/hazus/hz_casestudies.shtm	Emergency policy	Use of public institutions to respond to crisis	8	Research	Shows cases where agency was successful – strong bias
US Government Accountability Office	http://www.gao.gov/docsearch/featured/bp_reviews.html	Best practices, accountability, transparency	Best Practices Reviews identify other public and private sector organizations that are widely recognized for major improvements in their performance in a specific area, such as financial management. Show auditing and transparency initiatives at work	+10	Research	Government presentation of different audits used; best practices provide a model for other organizations with similar functions/missions

Title of Site	Address	Subject Areas	Relevance to Public Administration	No. of Cases	Potential Use of Cases	General Utility of Site
US Office of Personnel Management	http://www.opm.gov/studies/index.asp	Human resources management, e.g., performance measurement, leadership, incentives	Public management practices	+10	Training	Federal service training
Washington State Department of Ecology	http://www.ecy.wa.gov/pubs/topic.html	Environmental policy, mostly focused on Washington	Public policy	100+	Research	Government publications and reports produced by the Department of Ecology
Wisconsin State Department of Public Instruction	http://www.dpi.state.wi.us/dpi/dlsea/sspw/casestdy.html	Education policy	Designing educational programs and dealing with school policy issues	25+	Research into areas of public administration	Readers will benefit more from this document if they are familiar with an earlier publication, "Wisconsin's Framework for Comprehensive School Programs: An Integrated Approach"
Wisconsin Working Together Committee	http://workingtogether.state.wi.us		Publicly submitted case studies – no peer review process			
World Bank Institute Case Studies	http://web.worldbank.org/WBSITE/EXTERNAL/WBI/0,,contentMDK:20111575~menuPK:556286~pagePK:209023~piPK:207535~theSitePK:213799,00.html	Wide range of public administration issues	Public administration, management of public institutions	20+	Research	World Bank research exhibitions
Yale University: Program on Non-Profit Organizations (PONPO)	http://ponpo.som.yale.edu/publ.html	PONPO publishes the Cases on Non-Profit Governance Series	Public administration, and perspectives on the dynamics of non-profit governing boards	11	University training materials	A unique curricular resource

Bibliography

Akerly, M. "Supporting and Driving Collaboration with Web 2.0." Conference Board of Canada, May 2009.

Barnes, L. B., C. R. Christensen, and A. J. Hansen. *Teaching and the Case Method: Text, Cases, and Readings*. 3rd ed. Boston: Harvard Business School Press, 1994.

Batista, F. "Gestão do Conhecimento na Administração Pública" [Knowledge Management in Public Administration]. Brazil: IPEA, 2005.

Bruner, R. F., B. E. Gup, B. H. Nunnally, Jr., and L. C. Pettit. "Teaching with Cases to Graduate and Undergraduate Students." *Financial Practice and Education* 9, no. 2 (fall/winter 1999): 138-46.

Caceres, L., and S. Schwartz. "The Labour Market Experience of Recent Graduates from Masters Programs in Public Administration." School of Public Policy and Administration, Carleton University, Ottawa, July 2008. www.cappa.ca.

Christensen, C. R. *Teaching and the Case Method: Text, Cases and Readings*. Boston, MA: Harvard Business School, 1981.

Collins, M. "Embedded Systems Case Studies." Carnegie Mellon University, Pittsburgh, 1999. http://www.ece.cmu.edu/~koopman/des_s99/case_studies/index.html#role.

DeMichiell, R., R. Manning, and K. Reaves. "Teaching Ethics: A Case Study Approach." *International Journal of Case Method Research and Application* 17, no. 1 (2005): 8-22.

Duch, B. "Problems: A Key Factor in PBL." Center for Teaching Effectiveness, University of Delaware, 1997. http://www.udel.edu/pbl/cte/spr96-phys.html.

— "Characteristics of Good Problems. Center for Teaching Effectiveness, University of Delaware, 1997. http://www.udel.edu/pbl/cte/spr96-phys.html.

Duncan, D. *Clickers in the Classroom: How to Enhance Science Teaching Using Classroom Response Systems*. Pearson Education, 2005.

Eggers, W. D., and J. O'Leary. *If We Can Put a Man on the Moon . . . Getting Big Things Done in Government*. Boston: Harvard Business, 2009.

Eisenhardt, K. M. "Building Theories from Case Study Research." *Academy of Management Review* 14, no. 4 (1989): 352-550.

Ellet, W. *The Case Study Handbook: How to Read, Discuss, and Write Persuasively about Cases*. Boston: Harvard Business, 2007.

Emory, C. W., and D. R. Cooper. *Business Research Methods*. 4th ed. Boston, MA: Irvin, 1991.

Feagin, J. R., A. Orum, and G. Sjoberg, eds. *A Case for the Case Study*. Chapel Hill, NC: University of North Carolina Press, 1991.

Grayson H. Walker Teaching Resource Centre, University of Tennessee. "Underlying Procedures for Using Cases." Last modified April 16, 2002. http://www.utc.edu/Administration/WalkerTeachingResourceCenter/FacultyDevelopment/CaseTeaching/index.html.

Hamel, J., S. Dufour, and D. Fortin. *Case Study Methods*. Newbury Park, CA: Sage, 1993.

Herreid, C. F. "The Interrupted Case Method." *Journal of College Science Teaching* 35, no. 2 (2005): 4-5. http://www3.nsta.org/main/news/stories/college_science.php?news_story_ID=51003.

— "Jigsaw: A Case Study Technique Where Students Become Experts." National Center for Case Study Teaching in Science, University at Buffalo, State University of New York. http://ublib.buffalo.edu/libraries/projects/cases/teaching/jigsaw.html.

Kagan, D. M., and D. J. Tippins. "How Teachers' Classroom Cases Express Their Pedagogical Beliefs." *Journal of Teacher Education* 42, no. 4 (1991): 281-91.

Kim, O., B. J. Utke, and S. C., Hupp. "Comparing the Use of Case Studies and Application Questions in Preparing Special Education Professionals." *Teacher Education and Special Education* 28, no. 2 (2005): 104-113.

Kreber, C. "Learning Experientially through Case Studies? A Conceptual Analysis." *Teaching in Higher Education* 6, no. 2 (2001): 217-28.

Kunselman, J. C., and K. Johnson. "Using the Case Method to Facilitate Learning." *College Teaching* 52, no. 3 (2004): 92.

Kuntz, S., and A. Hesslar. "Bridging the Gap between Theory and Practice: Fostering Active Learning through the Case Method." Paper presented at the annual meeting of the Association of American Colleges and Universities, 1998.

Lawrence, P. R. "The Preparation of Case Material." In *The Case Method of Teaching Human Relations and Administration*, ed. K. R. Andrews. Cambridge, MA: Harvard University Press, 1953.

Levin, B. B. "Using the Case Method in Teacher Education: The Role of Discussion and Experience in Teachers' Thinking about Cases." *Teacher and Teacher Education* 11, no. 1 (1995): 63-79.

Lyons, N. "Teaching by the Case Method: One Teacher's Beginnings." *On Teaching and Learning: The Journal of the Harvard-Danforth Center* 3 (1989): 28-35.

Manning, M. "Teaching Ethics: A Case Study Approach with Project Management Methods." *International Journal of Case Method Research & Application* 17, no. 1 (2005): 8-22.

Martin, R. *The Opposable Mind*. Boston: Harvard Press, 2009.

McAninch, A. R. *Teacher Thinking and the Case Method: Theory and Future Directions*. New York: Teachers College Press, 1993.

McNaughton, D., T. E. Hall, and P. Maccini. "Case-Based Instruction in Special Education Teacher Preparation: Practices and Concerns of Teacher Educator/Researchers." *Teacher Education and Special Education* 24, no. 2 (2001): 84-94.

McNergney, J., et al. "Cooperation and Competition in Case-Based Teacher Education." *Journal of Teacher Education* 45, no. 5 (1994): 339-45.

Merseth, K. K. *The Case for Cases in Teacher Education*. Washington, DC: American Association for Higher Education, American Association of Colleges of Teacher Education, 1991.

Naumes, W., and M. Naumes. *The Art and Craft of Case Writing*. London: Sage, 1999.

Richards, L. G., M. Gorman, W. T. Scherer, and R. D. Landel. "Promoting Active Learning with Cases and Instructional Modules." *Journal of Engineering Education* 84, no. 4 (1995): 375-81.

Rogers, E. W. "Building a Healthy Learning Organization at NASA: Knowledge Management Systems as Human Systems." White paper. NASA/Goddard Space Flight Center, 2008.

Stake, R. E. *The Art of Case Study Research*. Thousand Oaks, CA: Sage, 1995.

Tellis, W. "Application of a Case Study Methodology." *The Qualitative Report* 3, no. 3 (September 1997). http://www.nova.edu/ssss/QR/QR3-3/tellis2.html.

Vilches Fresneda, P. S., and S. M. Goulart Gonçalves. *Formulating a Knowledge Management Policy Federal Public Administration: The Brazilian Experience*. Brazil: Chamber of Deputies, 2008.

Writing Case Studies: A Manual. Abridged version adapted for use by the Online Learning Centre. http://olc.spsd.sk.ca/de/pd/instr/strats/casestd/casestds.pdf.

Yemen, G. *On Writing Cases Well*. Charlottesville, VA: University of Virginia Darden School Foundation, 2006.

Yin, R. K. *Case Study Research: Design and Methods*. Newbury Park, CA: Sage, 1984.

Author's Biography

Andrew Graham researches, teaches, and writes on public sector management, financial management, integrated risk management and governance. He teaches at Queen's University School of Policy Studies as well as the Canadian Police College and a variety of international and Canadian venues. He is Series Editor of the Case Study Program of the Institute of Public Administration of Canada, Canada's leading source of public sector case studies.

He has published the first textbook on managing public money, entitled *Canadian Public-Sector Financial Management*, available through McGill-Queen's University Press. The text has been adopted by a number of Canada's leading universities.

Mr. Graham teaches in the graduate and professional development programs at Queen's and elsewhere. He also writes extensively, and is contributing a regular column on management issues, "Briefly Noted," for *Public Sector Management*, a periodical of the Institute of Public Administration of Canada.

Mr. Graham has taken a special interest in emerging management issues, including strategic planning, modern police governance, performance measurement, and integrated risk management. He has written extensively in these areas, including an e-book on the implementation of integrated risk management, available on his website. He is associated with the Building Democracy in Ukraine Project of Queen's University, a member of the advisory committee of the Centre for the Study of Democracy at Queen's, and Project Lead for the Queen's partnership in the Canada-Brazil Technical Co-operation Project.

An Assistant Deputy Minister for 14 years in the federal government with over 30 years of service, Mr. Graham also has experience in leading front-line (Warden, Kingston Penitentiary) and complex regional operations. He has held a number of policy and corporate leadership roles, including Senior Deputy Commissioner of the Correctional Service of Canada. He has extensive corporate management experience, including having served as the Assistant Deputy Minister, Corporate Services of Agriculture and Agri-Food Canada.

Mr. Graham served as president of APEX, the professional association of public executives. He is a voting member of the Institute on Governance, and a member of the editorial board of the *Canadian Public Administration Journal* of the Institute of Public Administration of Canada. He took part in an executive interchange to the Conference Board of Canada for two years.

Mr. Graham has a master's degree in political economy from the University of Toronto and a bachelor's degree from Glendon College, York University. He is a graduate of the Advanced Management Program of the Canadian Centre for Management Development.

He also holds a diploma in Landscape Design and Horticulture from Guelph University, and is a graduate of the Orvis School of Fly Fishing. Mr. Graham is vice-chair of the Frontenac Arch Biosphere Network, and a member of the Friends of Charleston Lake Park and Thousand Island Watershed Land Trust executives.

Queen's Policy Studies
Recent Publications

The Queen's Policy Studies Series is dedicated to the exploration of major public policy issues that confront governments and society in Canada and other nations.

Manuscript submission. We are pleased to consider new book proposals and manuscripts. Preliminary enquiries are welcome. A subvention is normally required for the publication of an academic book. Please direct questions or proposals to the Publications Unit by email at spspress@queensu.ca, or visit our website at: www.queensu.ca/sps/books, or contact us by phone at (613) 533-2192.

Our books are available from good bookstores everywhere, including the Queen's University bookstore (http://www.campusbookstore.com/). McGill-Queen's University Press is the exclusive world representative and distributor of books in the series. A full catalogue and ordering information may be found on their web site (http://mqup.mcgill.ca/).

School of Policy Studies

Canada's Isotope Crisis: What Next? Jatin Nathwani and Donald Wallace (eds.), 2010. Paper 978-1-55339-283-5 Cloth 978-1-55339-284-2

Pursuing Higher Education in Canada: Economic, Social, and Policy Dimensions, Ross Finnie, Marc Frenette, Richard E. Mueller, and Arthur Sweetman (eds.), 2010. Paper 978-1-55339-277-4 Cloth 978-1-55339-278-1

Canadian Immigration: Economic Evidence for a Dynamic Policy Environment, Ted McDonald, Elizabeth Ruddick, Arthur Sweetman, and Christopher Worswick (eds.), 2010. Paper 978-1-55339-281-1 Cloth 978-1-55339-282-8

Taking Stock: Research on Teaching and Learning in Higher Education, Julia Christensen Hughes and Joy Mighty (eds.), 2010. Paper 978-1-55339-271-2 Cloth 978-1-55339-272-9

Architects and Innovators: Building the Department of Foreign Affairs and International Trade, 1909–2009/Architectes et innovateurs : le développement du ministère des Affaires étrangères et du Commerce international,de 1909 à 2009, Greg Donaghy and Kim Richard Nossal (eds.), 2009. Paper 978-1-55339-269-9 Cloth 978-1-55339-270-5

Academic Transformation: The Forces Reshaping Higher Education in Ontario, Ian D. Clark, Greg Moran, Michael L. Skolnik, and David Trick, 2009. Paper 978-1-55339-238-5 Cloth 978-1-55339-265-1

The New Federal Policy Agenda and the Voluntary Sector: On the Cutting Edge, Rachel Laforest (ed.), 2009. Paper 978-1-55339-132-6

Measuring What Matters in Peace Operations and Crisis Management, Sarah Jane Meharg, 2009. Paper 978-1-55339-228-6 Cloth ISBN 978-1-55339-229-3

International Migration and the Governance of Religious Diversity, Paul Bramadat and Matthias Koenig (eds.), 2009. Paper 978-1-55339-266-8 Cloth ISBN 978-1-55339-267-5

Who Goes? Who Stays? What Matters? Accessing and Persisting in Post-Secondary Education in Canada, Ross Finnie, Richard E. Mueller, Arthur Sweetman, and Alex Usher (eds.), 2008. Paper 978-1-55339-221-7 Cloth ISBN 978-1-55339-222-4

Economic Transitions with Chinese Characteristics: Thirty Years of Reform and Opening Up, Arthur Sweetman and Jun Zhang (eds.), 2009. Paper 978-1-55339-225-5 Cloth ISBN 978-1-55339-226-2

Economic Transitions with Chinese Characteristics: Social Change During Thirty Years of Reform, Arthur Sweetman and Jun Zhang (eds.), 2009.
Paper 978-1-55339-234-7 Cloth ISBN 978-1-55339-235-4

Dear Gladys: Letters from Over There, Gladys Osmond (Gilbert Penney ed.), 2009.
Paper ISBN 978-1-55339-223-1

Immigration and Integration in Canada in the Twenty-first Century, John Biles, Meyer Burstein, and James Frideres (eds.), 2008.
Paper ISBN 978-1-55339-216-3 Cloth ISBN 978-1-55339-217-0

Robert Stanfield's Canada, Richard Clippingdale, 2008. ISBN 978-1-55339-218-7

Exploring Social Insurance: Can a Dose of Europe Cure Canadian Health Care Finance? Colleen Flood, Mark Stabile, and Carolyn Tuohy (eds.), 2008.
Paper ISBN 978-1-55339-136-4 Cloth ISBN 978-1-55339-213-2

Canada in NORAD, 1957–2007: A History, Joseph T. Jockel, 2007.
Paper ISBN 978-1-55339-134-0 Cloth ISBN 978-1-55339-135-7

Canadian Public-Sector Financial Management, Andrew Graham, 2007.
Paper ISBN 978-1-55339-120-3 Cloth ISBN 978-1-55339-121-0

Emerging Approaches to Chronic Disease Management in Primary Health Care, John Dorland and Mary Ann McColl (eds.), 2007.
Paper ISBN 978-1-55339-130-2 Cloth ISBN 978-1-55339-131-9

Fulfilling Potential, Creating Success: Perspectives on Human Capital Development, Garnett Picot, Ron Saunders and Arthur Sweetman (eds.), 2007.
Paper ISBN 978-1-55339-127-2 Cloth ISBN 978-1-55339-128-9

Reinventing Canadian Defence Procurement: A View from the Inside, Alan S. Williams, 2006.
Paper ISBN 0-9781693-0-1 (Published in association with Breakout Educational Network)

SARS in Context: Memory, History, Policy, Jacalyn Duffin and Arthur Sweetman (eds.), 2006. Paper ISBN 978-0-7735-3194-9 Cloth ISBN 978-0-7735-3193-2
(Published in association with McGill-Queen's University Press)

Dreamland: How Canada's Pretend Foreign Policy has Undermined Sovereignty, Roy Rempel, 2006. Paper ISBN 1-55339-118-7 Cloth ISBN 1-55339-119-5
(Published in association with Breakout Educational Network)

Canadian and Mexican Security in the New North America: Challenges and Prospects, Jordi Díez (ed.), 2006. Paper ISBN 978-1-55339-123-4 Cloth ISBN 978-1-55339-122-7

Global Networks and Local Linkages: The Paradox of Cluster Development in an Open Economy, David A. Wolfe and Matthew Lucas (eds.), 2005.
Paper ISBN 1-55339-047-4 Cloth ISBN 1-55339-048-2

Choice of Force: Special Operations for Canada, David Last and Bernd Horn (eds.), 2005.
Paper ISBN 1-55339-044-X Cloth ISBN 1-55339-045-8

Centre for the Study of Democracy

The Authentic Voice of Canada: R.B. Bennett's Speeches in the House of Lords, 1941-1947, Christopher McCreery and Arthur Milnes (eds.), 2009.
Paper 978-1-55339-275-0 Cloth ISBN 978-1-55339-276-7

Age of the Offered Hand: The Cross-Border Partnership Between President George H.W. Bush and Prime-Minister Brian Mulroney, A Documentary History, James McGrath and Arthur Milnes (eds.), 2009. Paper ISBN 978-1-55339-232-3
Cloth ISBN 978-1-55339-233-0

In Roosevelt's Bright Shadow: Presidential Addresses About Canada from Taft to Obama in Honour of FDR's 1938 Speech at Queen's University, Christopher McCreery and Arthur Milnes (eds.), 2009. Paper ISBN 978-1-55339-230-9 Cloth ISBN 978-1-55339-231-6

Politics of Purpose, 40th Anniversary Edition, The Right Honourable John N. Turner 17th Prime Minister of Canada, Elizabeth McIninch and Arthur Milnes (eds.), 2009. Paper ISBN 978-1-55339-227-9 Cloth ISBN 978-1-55339-224-8

Bridging the Divide: Religious Dialogue and Universal Ethics, Papers for The InterAction Council, Thomas S. Axworthy (ed.), 2008. Paper ISBN 978-1-55339-219-4 Cloth ISBN 978-1-55339-220-0

Institute of Intergovernmental Relations

Canada: The State of the Federation 2009, vol. 22, *Carbon Pricing and Environmental Federalism*, Thomas J. Courchene and John R. Allan (eds.), 2010. Paper ISBN 978-1-55339-196-8 Cloth ISBN 978-1-55339-197-5

Canada: The State of the Federation 2008, vol. 21, *Open Federalism and the Spending Power*, Thomas J. Courchene, John R. Allan, and Hoi Kong (eds.), forthcoming. Paper ISBN 978-1-55339-194-4

The Democratic Dilemma: Reforming the Canadian Senate, Jennifer Smith (ed.), 2009. Paper 978-1-55339-190-6

Canada: The State of the Federation 2006/07, vol. 20, *Transitions – Fiscal and Political Federalism in an Era of Change*, John R. Allan, Thomas J. Courchene, and Christian Leuprecht (eds.), 2009. Paper ISBN 978-1-55339-189-0 Cloth ISBN 978-1-55339-191-3

Comparing Federal Systems, Third Edition, Ronald L. Watts, 2008. Paper ISBN 978-1-55339-188-3

Canada: The State of the Federation 2005, vol. 19, *Quebec and Canada in the New Century – New Dynamics, New Opportunities*, Michael Murphy (ed.), 2007. Paper ISBN 978-1-55339-018-3 Cloth ISBN 978-1-55339-017-6

Spheres of Governance: Comparative Studies of Cities in Multilevel Governance Systems, Harvey Lazar and Christian Leuprecht (eds.), 2007. Paper ISBN 978-1-55339-019-0 Cloth ISBN 978-1-55339-129-6

Canada: The State of the Federation 2004, vol. 18, *Municipal-Federal-Provincial Relations in Canada*, Robert Young and Christian Leuprecht (eds.), 2006. Paper ISBN 1-55339-015-6 Cloth ISBN 1-55339-016-4

Canadian Fiscal Arrangements: What Works, What Might Work Better, Harvey Lazar (ed.), 2005. Paper ISBN 1-55339-012-1 Cloth ISBN 1-55339-013-X

Canada: The State of the Federation 2003, vol. 17, *Reconfiguring Aboriginal-State Relations*, Michael Murphy (ed.), 2005. Paper ISBN 1-55339-010-5 Cloth ISBN 1-55339-011-3

Queen's Centre for International Relations

Europe Without Soldiers? Recruitment and Retention across the Armed Forces of Europe, Tibor Szvircsev Tresch and Christian Leuprecht (eds.), 2010. Paper 978-1-55339-246-0 Cloth ISBN 978-1-55339-247-7

Mission Critical: Smaller Democracies' Role in Global Stability Operations, Christian Leuprecht, Jodok Troy, and David Last (eds.), 2010. Paper 978-1-55339-244-6

The Afghanistan Challenge: Hard Realities and Strategic Choices, Hans-Georg Ehrhart and Charles Pentland (eds.), 2009. Paper 978-1-55339-241-5

John Deutsch Institute for the Study of Economic Policy

The 2009 Federal Budget: Challenge, Response and Retrospect, Charles M. Beach, Bev Dahlby and Paul A.R. Hobson (eds.), 2010.
Paper ISBN 978-1-55339-165-4 Cloth ISBN 978-1-55339-166-1

Discount Rates for the Evaluation of Public Private Partnerships, David F. Burgess and Glenn P. Jenkins (eds.), 2010. Paper ISBN 978-1-55339-163-0 Cloth ISBN 978-1-55339-164-7

Retirement Policy Issues in Canada, Michael G. Abbott, Charles M. Beach, Robin W. Boadway, and James G. MacKinnon (eds.), 2009.
Paper ISBN 978-1-55339-161-6 Cloth ISBN 978-1-55339-162-3

The 2006 Federal Budget: Rethinking Fiscal Priorities, Charles M. Beach, Michael Smart, and Thomas A. Wilson (eds.), 2007. Paper ISBN 978-1-55339-125-8
Cloth ISBN 978-1-55339-126-6

Health Services Restructuring in Canada: New Evidence and New Directions, Charles M. Beach, Richard P. Chaykowksi, Sam Shortt, France St-Hilaire, and Arthur Sweetman (eds.), 2006. Paper ISBN 978-1-55339-076-3
Cloth ISBN 978-1-55339-075-6

A Challenge for Higher Education in Ontario, Charles M. Beach (ed.), 2005.
Paper ISBN 1-55339-074-1 Cloth ISBN 1-55339-073-3

Current Directions in Financial Regulation, Frank Milne and Edwin H. Neave (eds.), Policy Forum Series no. 40, 2005. Paper ISBN 1-55339-072-5 Cloth ISBN 1-55339-071-7

Higher Education in Canada, Charles M. Beach, Robin W. Boadway, and R. Marvin McInnis (eds.), 2005. Paper ISBN 1-55339-070-9 Cloth ISBN 1-55339-069-5
